THE PSYCHOTHERAPIST'S GUIDE TO COST CONTAINMENT

THE PSYCHOTHERAPIST'S GUIDE TO COST CONTAINMENT

How to Survive and Thrive
in an Age of Managed Care

Bernard D. Beitman, M.D.

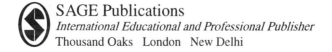
SAGE Publications
International Educational and Professional Publisher
Thousand Oaks London New Delhi

For information:

SAGE Publications, Inc.
2455 Teller Road
Thousand Oaks, California 91320
E-mail: order@sagepub.com

SAGE Publications Ltd.
6 Bonhill Street
London EC2A 4PU
United Kingdom

SAGE Publications India Pvt. Ltd.
M-32 Market
Greater Kailash I
New Delhi 110 048 India

Printed in the United States of America

Library of Congress Cataloging-in-Publication Data

Beitman, Bernard D.
    The psychotherapist's guide to cost containment: How to survive
and thrive in an age of managed care / by Bernard D. Beitman.
        p. cm.
    Includes bibliographical references and index.
    ISBN 0-8039-7381-0 (cloth: acid-free paper)
    ISBN 0-8039-7382-9 (pbk.: acid-free paper)
    1. Managed mental health care. 2. Psychotherapy—Practice.
I. Title.
RC465.5.B455 1998
616.89'14'068—dc21   97-33921

This book is printed on acid-free paper.

98 99 00 01 02 03 10 9 8 7 6 5 4 3 2 1

Acquiring Editor:	Jim Nageotte
Editorial Assistant:	Kathleen Derby
Production Editor:	Sanford Robinson
Production Assistant:	Lynn Miyata
Typesetter/Designer:	Janelle LeMaster
Indexer:	Teri Greenberg
Cover Designer:	Candice Harman
Print Buyer:	Anna Chin

Contents

Preface

The times have changed for psychotherapists. A century ago, Freud's *The Interpretation of Dreams* (1900/1953) helped initiate the American delight in self-examination. His consulting room, private and confidential, modeled the solo practitioner of the last half of the 20th century. As we prepare to enter the 21st century, American psychotherapy has become industrialized as cottage industry office-centered practitioners find themselves swept up in massive economic and organizational change. The lure of psychotherapy remains—its journey into self-discovery, its window into the emotional depths of culture and humanity—yet more than any new school of therapy, the health care economic revolution is reshaping its theory and its practice. Benefit can accompany change, opportunity can be found in crisis, and learning can come from adversity. Psychotherapy can learn from these arduous times, and therapists can find hope in the sheer power of these changes. First, the nature of the new economic beast must be understood in order to tame it.

This book's title includes "cost containment" because containing costs is only the first step in realizing the ideals toward which the revolution is lurching. Managed care organizations (MCOs) utilize a host of tools to achieve this aim, some more like hammers, others more like scalpels (Chapter 1), but they can and do take on a human face (Chapter

2). Nevertheless, much fear and much anger is being generated in therapists because they see their livelihoods clearly being threatened and their ability to care for their clients frighteningly impeded. To understand these ugly forces, one must look at the industrialization of mental health treatment, yet another wave in the massive industrial revolution begun in 18th century England. Corporate-think, business plans, downsizing, and labor unions are invading the psychotherapist's private thoughts (Chapter 3) and playing havoc with some of our most cherished ethical (Chapter 4), treatment, and educational (Chapter 5) ideals.

Much can be done. We must trumpet the efficacy and effectiveness of psychotherapy. We must confront the problems lying both within and outside the health care system (Chapter 6). We must step outside our offices into the medical, self-group, and political systems that call for our input and expertise (Chapter 7). We must look for opportunistic ways to survive (Chapter 8). Finally, we must recognize how much managed care, more than any single influence since psychoanalysis, has redefined psychotherapy (Chapter 9).

Much of your reaction to these changes depends upon your perspective, upon your economic position, and your longevity as a therapist.

If you are an *academic* psychotherapist, you may view the cost containment movement as simply another interesting political event. This book points out the tremendous impact it will soon have on your students who aspire to clinical practice.

If you are a *graduate student,* you may be wondering whether you should try to be a clinician with a psychotherapeutic focus. You may find that your teachers do not know much about how to practice in the new economic environment. To be credentialed in managed care organizations requires experience, licenses, and certificates as well as the right contacts. Beginners may need to start fast, develop many options, and be willing to work long hours for relatively little money. This book describes what you will need to know to accelerate your psychotherapeutic career.

If you are an *early career practitioner*, you probably are studying the trends and taking action to achieve and maintain a satisfactory balance between your business and your personal life. You may be prepared to earn a lower income than your older colleagues had enjoyed. This book presents the emerging principles of managed care that you will need to know to take the calculated risks now required for your success.

If you are a *mature practitioner*, the troubling times may force early retirement. On the other hand, your experiences and your firmly established referral networks may provide you an opportunity to create new systems to compete in the new marketplace. Some of your colleagues have created their own companies. If you are near retirement age and have other sources of income, you may be able simply to sit back, run a limited psychotherapy practice, and be glad you do not have to adapt. You may find what is written here and going on around you to be interesting. On the other hand, with little to lose, you may wish to take some risks, using your experience, savvy, and connections to create something uniquely yours in these turbulent times. This book will help you to outline the parameters you will need to take into consideration.

This book is intended to help therapists of all professions and of all schools to blunt the sharp forces of cost containment and to chart a hopeful path toward enabling psychotherapists once again to take responsibility with their clients for making the decisions that optimize psychotherapeutic care.

Acknowledgments

To struggle through the massive number of fluctuating ideas surrounding both the revolution in health care financing and psychotherapy practice requires the help of many others. I am grateful to Sam Bradshaw, D. Brown, Les Bryant, Rick Burch, Bob Churchill, Kay Davis, Tom Eppright, Rich Erwin, Barb Foos, Marvin Goldfried, Al Greimann, Patsy Hart, Cheryl Hemme, Arshad Husain, Frank Mitchell, John Norcross, Jerry Parker, Jim Slaughter, Mike Sundall, Andrew Weil, and Dongmei Yue. Thanks also to the many psychiatric residents at the University of Missouri-Columbia who have taught me about psychotherapy as I have attempted to teach them. The best teachers are ones whose names cannot be mentioned—my patients.

One also must be mindful of the many pitfalls an author faces. Helping me to keep my mind on the target were my sons, Karlen Beitman and Arie Beitman, and my wife, Paula Levine.

And thank you, Debby Burnley, for your patient secretarial perfections.

Jim Nageotte, my editor at Sage, helped to transform an undirected proposal into a focused and, I hope, highly useful volume.

COST CONTAINMENT

The requisite knowledge base for psychotherapists has increased several-fold. Pressures to contain medical care costs prompted the evolution of a collection of tools far removed from cognitive restructuring, interpretations, exposure, and reframing. Directly and indirectly, these tools, utilized by the large payers including governments and businesses through their managed care organizations (MCOs), strongly influence the conduct of psychotherapy. Chapter 1 outlines these proliferating constraints and describes the new organizational structures (HMOs, PPOs, IPAs, PSNs) that are evolving to implement the drive for cost containment with the use of these new tools.

Therapists have several options for survival; lowest on the list of possibilities lies solo private practice unless a means is found to disengage from the managed care juggernaut. Most therapists will find their way into some kind of organizational structure either created by colleagues as described in Chapter 2 or by a regional or national managed care company.

Major battle lines are forming. Providers have become Labor, however professional our titles. Managed care organizations and their employers, the major payers, have become Management. The Industrial Revolution, based upon new technologies and the organization of labor, has come to health care and to psychotherapy as described in Chapter 3. But care cannot be sold like toothpaste! The ideal future for this revolution is not limited only to cost containment. It must evolve into managing of care and ultimately into the managing of physical and mental health together.

Tools of Cost Containment

Managed care organizations (MCOs) have sprung into existence because they provide a much desired service: They act as mediators between the providers of service (therapists, physicians, and other health care providers) and payers (business and government). Payers reap benefits from cost savings, MCOs make profits from administrative overhead and cost containment, most therapists experience static or reduced income, and most clients in managed care systems experience limitations on choice of therapist and number of visits. How deleterious these results are to populations being served remains a mystery because research to answer this question has not accompanied the implementation of this experiment. Ideally, MCOs will help to manage care, not just cost; it is hoped that MCOs will help to manage the health of a population being served. Cost containment, however, remains the primary objective of the managed care movement. Quality, very difficult to measure in psychotherapy, is only slowly and in fits and starts becoming a secondary objective.

Managed care companies can make profits for themselves and their shareholders by excluding the highest-risk clients and the highest-cost physicians. Before managed care, health insurance companies acted with similar economic self-interest. MCOs maximize profits through a simple formula: Take in as much money as possible through monthly insurance premiums, and limit the amount of money going out for treatment. The best way to accomplish this end is to insure the well and to limit payments for the sick. Insurance company statistics indicate that approximately 20% of the insured account for 80% of the payments made; therefore, companies strive to insure the 80% who use small amounts of treatment and to avoid insuring the 20% who are high utilizers. Such managed care schemers have provided some MCOs up to 30% of every premium dollar for marketing, administration, and profit.

BENEFIT PLAN DESIGNS

Benefit designs refer to the agreements between payers and MCOs defining the benefits to be offered beneficiaries. A weak mental health benefit provides the simplest way to reduce mental health costs. The terms *medical management* and *management program* refer to the types of activities that managed care companies use to control cost and assess the quality of the health services they provide to their populations (Touse, 1993). These efforts can be placed under three general categories: (a) utilization management, (b) quality assurance, and (c) dispute resolution procedures. Once under the clear control of providers, utilization and quality assurance are increasingly coming under external scrutiny.

The psychotherapy benefits actually available to plan members depend on the amount of money allocated for behavioral health. In 1990, Americans spent approximately 10% of their health care dollars on mental health treatments, while many managed care companies, through the payers' benefit plan decisions, allocated 3-5% (Iglehart, 1996) or less. A survey of 40 of the largest employee-assistance and managed behavioral health companies found that they allocated an average of $5 per member per month (pmpm) (Iglehart, 1996). (The designation "per member per month" is a commonly accepted way to calculate payments by payers and MCOs for various benefit plan services.) In 1996, the pmpm ranged from about $1.50 to $4.50 (not including benefit plans for the severely and persistently mentally ill, which have much higher pmpm costs).

The coverage limits and incentives of benefit designs mark the outlines within which an MCO manages treatment. Managed care plans, like their predecessor plans, tend to discriminate against mental health treatments by restricting coverage and incorporating disincentives to seek care, such as requiring high copayments each time service is sought by clients (Anderson & Berlant, 1993) or by eliminating mental health benefits.

Coverage Limits

Plans limit benefits in several ways to protect the payer and/or MCO from unlimited losses. Limits may be structured in several ways.

1. Levels of care: A major problem with previous insurance coverage was its tendency to pay too much for inpatient treatment but very little for outpatient. Managed care has reversed this discrepancy by placing increasing emphasis on outpatient treatment. A large source of profit for MCOs and cost savings for payers has been realized through reducing inpatient psychiatric and substance abuse utilization (Hersch, 1994).
2. Day/dollar limits: An unpublished 1991 report described the following limits for mental health/substance abuse (MH/SA) (Anderson & Berlant, 1993):

   a. Deductibles: $500 per individual and $1,200 per family
   b. Mental health annual limit: $6,000
   c. Substance abuse annual limit: $8,000
   d. Lifetime MH/SA: $125,000

   Another common limit regards outpatient days and inpatient days: 20 outpatient visits and 30 inpatient visits. Employees/ patients often read these limits as their right and are surprised to learn that these are upper limits that may never be reached if MCO case managers refuse to authorize continued treatments.
3. Types of disorders: Many plans limit coverage to certain types of problems. Sexual dysfunction and obesity, among others, are often excluded, as are personality disorders. Usually the benefit limit makes treatment of disorders like anorexia extremely difficult because many more than 10-20 sessions are often necessary.
4. Types of treatment: Plans usually limit the number of days for inpatient treatment and the number of outpatient sessions.

Many plans exclude biofeedback and electroconvulsive therapies despite clear evidence of the usefulness of these procedures.

5. Types of providers: The earlier indemnity insurance plans often limited coverage to MDs and PhDs, but MCOs have lately recognized the difficulty in demonstrating the outcome differences correlated with individual professions and have supported payment to the less expensive and less extensively trained master's level providers (such as social workers and marriage and family counselors). Some plans specifically exclude psychiatrists from doing psychotherapy and permit PhDs to work with only a limited group of psychotherapy candidates.

Disincentives for Treatment

MCOs place several barriers in the way of people seeking psychotherapy, including high copayments and gatekeepers. Several studies have demonstrated that persons seeking mental health treatment are strongly influenced by the amount of the copayment associated with each psychotherapy visit (e.g., Simon, Grothaus, Durham, VonKorff, & Pabiniak, 1996). Copayment is the fee directly paid by the client at the time of service, either a fixed fee, often $5-$15, or a percentage of the unit cost, such as 10% of a $90 session fee. If, for example, a fixed copayment is raised from $10 to $15, clients are likely to reduce their frequency of visits or seek another provider with a smaller copayment.

Benefit plans often permit the option of wider choice through Point of Service (POS) plans but require a significantly higher copayment. POS, a confusing misnomer, refers to plans that permit clients to receive psychotherapy with providers who are outside the major network but still formally associated with the plan whose inclusion offers greater choice. Greater choice means greater cost.

Benefit plans rarely publish their lists of providers, thereby requiring members to pass through a gatekeeper. These gatekeepers offer the services of a wide variety of therapists and try to know who is best for specific problems. In addition, they refer members to providers who are likely to follow the MCO rules. Many plans use primary care physicians as gatekeepers. Although the concept of a primary care physician seems desirable and can be effective, in practice this system offers just one more hurdle for the therapy-seeking client to overcome. These hurdles can be very forbidding, as illustrated in the following example:

> A physical therapist working in our hospital had become very anxious. Her primary care physician was also a colleague who sent her client referrals. Her sleep had been disturbed for almost a year by worries about her children and job. When a friend suggested she seek some mental health assistance, she declined, saying "I don't want my primary care physician to know I don't have my life all together." This professional affiliation with her primary care physician prevented her from seeking psychotherapeutic help. Had she not had this barrier to psychotherapy, she would likely have gone for help.

UTILIZATION REVIEW, MANAGEMENT, AND REPORTING

MCOs have identified several highly effective treatment review mechanisms by which to control the costs of medical and mental health treatment. These methods continue to evolve and become sharpened in order to continue the process of cost reduction and revenue enhancement. These methods include utilization review, utilization management, and utilization reporting.

Utilization Review (UR)

After an increasing number of MCOs had established nonspecialized staffs to review general medicine cases, the companies realized that mental health utilization review required specialized training. The forward-thinking companies either developed their own mental health and substance abuse reviewers or contracted with companies specializing in this area. Unfortunately, some companies hired poorly trained reviewers or instructed their reviewers to say "no!" as often as possible, denying needed services.

Preadmission certification remains the cornerstone of UR because hospital bed days cost more than any other single unit in MH/SA expenditures. As managed care evolves, it is likely that "medical necessity" for inpatient treatment will require danger to self or to others; any other compelling reason for hospitalization will not suffice. Taking the place of inpatient treatment, full continua of care are developing to treat clients outside the hospital setting using day treatment, case management, and home visits.

In most systems, UR reviewers are also involved with *prior authorization* of outpatient treatment, whether psychotherapy, medication management, or some other. A reviewer must approve any and all outpatient visits *before* the therapist will receive reimbursement. The same UR staff keeps regular contact with providers to limit the number of inpatient days or psychotherapy sessions through *concurrent review*.

Utilization Management (UM)

Utilization management incorporates UR but goes further to find the best match between treatment and provider for each client problem by considering the course of the client's illness. UM strives for optimal client care and cost savings. To be effective, UM requires that a system be developed for directing cases to the most appropriate case manager. For example, a client with several medical problems should be referred to a mental health nurse rather than a social worker, and substance abuse cases should be referred to a manager with such experience.

Successful UM systems possess quality screens that identify providers with the best practice patterns for specific problems, as well as detecting defects in quality. For example, a provider may be attempting psychotherapy with a severely depressed client when pharmacotherapy might be indicated. Some therapists may perform better with bulimics, whereas others may have greater success with anxiety disorders.

The fundamentals of utilization management include the following:

- Promoting correct diagnosis and effective treatment by assisting plan members to find access to the best kind of treatment. Utilization review (UR) simply works to deny unnecessarily intense treatment.

- Preventing recidivism by monitoring interepisode well-being and encouraging interepisode treatment where warranted (Anderson & Berlant, 1993).

Utilization Reporting

Some clients overutilize resources. Some companies explore their databases to find those clients incurring high costs and with extensive medical records. These companies target those clients for careful utilization evaluation and management targeted to reduce their high utilization.

REFERRAL MANAGEMENT
THROUGH GATEKEEPERS

Costs also can be controlled by directing the help-seeking plan member to a cost-effective provider rather than permitting random chance, whim, or even reputation to guide the selection. MCOs have devised a number of different mechanisms by which to direct clients to providers they believe to be optimal. Most channeling mechanisms involve some kind of gatekeeper, such as employee assistance programs (EAP), primary care physicians (PCP), and 1-800 case managers who specialize in mental health and substance abuse evaluation. Channeling can reduce cost in several ways: (a) disincentives to seek any psychotherapy treatment, (b) referral to cost-conscious psychotherapists who limit the number of sessions, and (c) referral to high-quality, cost-effective therapists who provide high value and help reduce relapse.

Employee Assistance Programs
as Gatekeeper

Employee assistance programs (EAPs) play unique roles in corporate America by serving as easily accessible entry points for employees and dependents with a variety of problems. EAPs generally advertise themselves as the first and most discreet source of help for marital and family problems, emotional problems, drug and alcohol abuse, work difficulties, and legal and financial difficulties. EAPs also work directly for employers. If, for example, Charles is not functioning well at work, his supervisor might ask him to be evaluated by an EAP counselor to determine the source of the difficulty. Employer-referred consultations are not necessarily confidential because the employer, not the employee, is the primary customer. The EAP provider attempts to find ways to help Charles resolve the difficulty and reports back to his supervisor. The report may become part of his record. EAPs also may serve the employee directly as the primary customer. When the employee is the primary customer, then confidentiality guidelines apply. Many EAPs offer short-term psychotherapy for relatively minor problems; when necessary, some clients are referred on for higher levels of professional care. The EAP staff is not usually penalized for referring on, nor are they financially rewarded for preventing a referral. Mature systems tie EAP activities to financial incentives.

EAPs provide valuable services because they can help people early in the course of a problem, often preventing it from progressing. On the other hand, EAP staff are not always clinically credentialed and qualified. Most lack the ability to distinguish between a psychopharmacologically responsive disorder and a psychotherapeutically responsive one, or one that might require a combination of treatment.

Primary Care Physician (PCP)
as Gatekeeper

Many managed care plans limit access to specialists, including psychotherapists, by requiring prior approval by the primary care physician before any specialist, including a mental health professional, may be consulted. Increasingly, programs are encouraging PCPs to diagnose and treat uncomplicated mental health problems. PCPs, well known for their weaknesses in identifying and treating behavioral problems (Mechanic, 1990), respond idiosyncratically to this demand. Some PCPs prefer to specialize in OB-GYN, others in cardiology, others in infectious disease, and still others in psychosocial difficulties. The client care justification for requiring PCPs as gatekeepers is based on the ideal of one physician managing the care of each client, perhaps a longing for the past, when the family doctor played the central medical role in many communities. The large number of persons assigned to PCPs, however, makes the evolution of close, personal relationships unlikely. Instead, clients seeking mental health professionals find themselves tracking down the PCP to secure the required authorization, often without evaluation. On the other hand, many primary care practices include psychotherapists in their groups, often in the same location, making referrals and collaborative treatment much simpler and more effective.

Long-Distance Gatekeepers

MCO-paid telephone caseworkers can satisfactorily screen help-seekers to provide an appropriate match between client problem and therapist. Sometimes, the decision to refer to a specific provider may be based on the provider's close adherence to the company's treatment (and cost-containment) policies rather than quality of work.

Long-distance gatekeepers must authorize or deny additional sessions. Therapists must provide timely, detailed treatment plans to reviewers in other cities who are often slow to authorize or deny additional sessions. For example, the insurance clerk at the therapist's office could have been sick and did not fax with sufficient time before the next session. The therapist's fee might not be reimbursed because the session was not authorized *prior to* its being conducted, as is generally required.

Some MCOs gradually recognize the value of allowing direct and easy access to mental health services for its payoff in terms of early detection and treatment and thus prevention of a more disabling condition. In addition, members are likely to be more satisfied with a system that does not involve difficult hurdles. MCOs may be realizing that most psychotherapy clients utilize an average of four to eight sessions. After 16 years in operation, 80% of MCOs allowed direct access to mental health services (Anderson & Berlant, 1993).

Direct access can reduce client confusion. For example, the primary care physician who recommends mental health treatment may make suggestions to the client about the nature of the treatment to be expected. These suggestions may be helpful if the primary care system has a good understanding of the mental health system, in which case there is likely to be close overlap between physician-provided expectations and the reality of treatment. If, however, mental health treatment is disengaged from primary care, then the first few sessions may be spent disentangling the treatment plan expectations of the primary care physician from those of the therapist.

Local Gatekeepers

Some systems permit clients to be evaluated by a local mental health professional. The assessor refers to the most skilled therapist for this person's needs and concerns; ideally, the assessor knows the panel of potential therapists personally.

PROVIDER PAYMENT SCHEMES

MCOs negotiate providers into payment schemes that reduce payments to them. These mechanisms include withholds, decreasing payments for additional sessions, case rates, and capitation. Within these constraints, psychotherapists are expected to optimize their service effectiveness.

1. *Withholds.* Therapists practicing in a discounted fee-for-service format with a managed care organization may be required to allow the MCO to withhold approximately 15% of the agreed upon fee. In other words, if the discounted fee for psychotherapy is $70 per session, the provider is paid only $59.50, or 85% of the discounted fee. Although the MCO is operating under a fixed budget paid by the payer at the beginning of the year, therapists are operating under the scheme of fee per session.

At the end of the year, the company will determine how closely the provider network (of which the individual therapist is a part) approximated the projected annual allotment for the population the provider group was serving. If the provider group came in more than 15% higher, then the 15% is not returned. If the group came in at the amount paid by the payer at the beginning of the year, the 15% is returned. If the actual rate per member per month is between 15% and the targeted amount, then the withhold return is prorated accordingly.

2. *Decreasing payment for additional increments of service.* The more a therapist does for a specific client, the less the therapist is paid for each additional session. The first five sessions might be reimbursed for X dollars each, the next five for 80% of X, the next five for 50% of X, and the next five for 30% of X.

3. *Case rate.* A flat fee is offered per case. For example, if a plan has a 20-visit maximum therapy benefit, the MCO might offer a case rate of $550, meaning that no matter how many sessions the therapist used (whether 2 or 20), he or she is paid $550 for treating the case. Although case rates can seem like risky arrangements to many therapists, they offer providers a greater measure of control over treatment plan design. No longer does a provider have to seek approval for additional sessions from case managers; the therapist *becomes* the case manager.

4. *Assume capitation.* Capitation plays a central role in the new economics. Capitation refers to placing a dollar value on the services *to be rendered* in the subsequent year for each member of the population to be served. Capitation rates for mental health services range from about $1 per member per month for a very healthy population to $25 per member per month for a severely incapacitated group. From this upfront money, the MCO or therapist group must make its profit. If providers assume the capitation instead of being paid fee-for-service, they assume the financial risk. If the provider group is to make money, the group as a whole must make its total costs less than the prepaid annual sum. Providers then seek to reduce costs by subsuming the utilization management functions of the MCO into their own practice patterns.

Capitation implies that the vendor (the group wishing to provide services by contract) accepts payment per person covered by the plan per month in exchange for providing services. In a pure capitation contract, all financial risk rests with the MCO or the provider group. The MCO or provider-sponsored network (PSN) should be unwilling to make a low bid if it must bear all the risk. (A PSN is a group of psychotherapists who have banded together in a legal structure that permits them to act as a single entity in signing contracts and managing care.)

5. *Soft capitation (risk sharing).* Under this arrangement, the employer (payer) shares risk with the MCO. If C were the target per member per month (pmpm) cost under straight capitation, the MCO would be paid that amount and take all the risk. Under shared risk, the contract determines that the employer pays more if costs go above C and less if costs are below C according to an agreed upon formula. Risk sharing constrains profits and losses to the MCO. If, for example, claims costs fall below C, MCO profits may increase at a rate of 50% of the cost shortfall, up to a limit of 5% of the agreed upon target amount, C. Similarly, if actual costs go above C, net payments to the MCO will fall at a rate of 50% of the cost overrun, up to a limit of 5% of the target. The "risk corridor" over which an MCO or PSN can increase profits or experience losses is limited. Most of the risk is born by the employer (Frank, McGuire, & Newhouse, 1995).[1]

6. *Other incentive arrangements.* Reward systems based on client satisfaction and quality of care are being developed. MCOs may be asked to put a portion of their fee "at risk" if certain standards are not met,

such as those for phone answering speed, consumer satisfaction, effective network development, data accuracy, and claim payment to providers.

The major challenge of any capitation-based payment system is to reduce incentives to undertreat while increasing incentives to contain costs. An effective payment system will mix prospective (e.g., withholds) and retrospective (e.g., reimburse full capitation rate if standards are met) components in such a manner as to create incentives to economize while limiting profits from undertreatment.

Convincing data have demonstrated the cost savings associated with the reduction of inpatient utilization—using community and home resources instead—without any major negative effects on treatment outcome (Balas & Beitman, n.d.). No evidence is available, however, to suggest that restricted access to outpatient treatment results in significant cost savings *and* an increase in the quality of care. There may be, in fact, a decrease in quality (Iglehart, 1996). "Report cards" are being developed to reflect the major outcome variables, including access to care, client and provider satisfaction, quality of care, and treatment outcome. Payers may be looking for value as well as cost savings, but measurements of value remain controversial.

QUALITY MANAGEMENT OF PROVIDERS

MCOs manage their provider panels in several ways. (A panel refers to the list of psychotherapists eligible to accept referrals from a specific MCO.)

Provider Selection

The most powerful way to ensure high quality is to select the best providers. Although MCOs may act as if the criteria for high-quality providers are well established, there are still no criteria to use to identify the best match between psychotherapists and particular problems and clients. Current attempts at provider screening and monitoring may be based on unproven but face-valid criteria such as (a) years of experience, (b) areas of specialization, (c) type of degree, and (d) history of legal difficulties. More likely, unspoken screening criteria, such as the willingness of therapists to comply with cost-reducing attitudes, play a significant role. For example:

- All mental health practitioners must be capable of carrying out goal-directed, time-efficient psychotherapy; be experienced in multidisciplinary team work; and be willing to seek and accept peer group consultation.

- Psychiatrists must be willing to write prescriptions while others do psychotherapy and spend their greatest efforts with the most seriously disturbed.

- Doctorate psychologists must carefully decide when to do psychological testing and readily refer to psychiatrists and/or primary care physicians for evaluation of potentially medication-responsive diagnoses.

- Master's level social workers and psychologists must be comfortable working in conjunction with psychiatrists and must be knowledgeable about family systems interventions and community interventions.

- Master's level nurses must be knowledgeable about current psychopharmacology and have general medical nursing experience.

Whether these requirements yield optimal client care and value has yet to be demonstrated, but they are what many consider appropriate for many types of mental health professionals.

Provider Profiling

Systems for profiling therapists are created from indicators. Indicators are developed from claims and certification data accumulated by the MCO.

Utilization profiling measures the average number of visits per client (from the company perspective, the fewer the better) and the average number of visits per subscriber, where the subscriber is the business unit contracting for services. MCOs can use these data to influence therapists into cutting treatment short.

Outcome profiling offers a list of various outcome measures. These include the quality of therapist treatment reports as judged by clinicians at the managed care company, the diagnostic mix of clients (e.g., anxiety disorders vs. borderline clients vs. schizophrenics and their severity ratings), client satisfaction including direct complaints and praise, recidivism, relapse, medical insurance claims cost, symptom change (both medical and psychiatric), and client work status including absenteeism rates and possibly productivity measures.

Case manager ratings offer global estimates per contact of cost-effectiveness, quality of care, and cooperativeness with the managed care system. The value of this latter criterion cannot be underestimated. Case managers may be more likely to negatively bias ratings of a repeatedly angry therapist.

Chart audits focus on clients with an apparent excess of sessions, perhaps uncovering instances of poor treatment decisions. For example, a therapist may have missed substance abuse in the initial evaluation and misfocused treatment, or a child therapist may have failed to bring in the family for evaluation when that would have accelerated treatment response.

Information about each psychotherapy case is aggregated into a composite rating (a scorecard or report card grade) to reflect the therapist's compatibility with the managed care network. The indicators vary from company to company and occasionally are altered by legal action. Most companies emphasize cost savings. Some try to emphasize both high quality and cost savings. The greater the control that therapists acquire over the management of their own clients, the less money will go for managed care administration and the more will go for improving quality of care for the same cost. The danger of provider efficiency is that payers may seek their own cost savings from the potential profit of cost-efficient therapist groups.

Provider education is crucial to therapist adaptation to this new economic environment. Therapist education may be enhanced by the following methods.

- *Treatment protocols and critical pathways* are being developed for mental health treatments, as they are for some aspects of general medicine. Providers may be monitored for compliance with these guidelines. The necessary investment in research to develop these protocols has yet to be made, although guidelines have been prepared for some disorders, including depression (Vibbert & Youngs, 1995) and bipolar disorder.

- *Peer review* offers a potentially effective means by which to improve treatment patterns by requiring regular staff meetings to
review both complex and simple cases. Complex cases tend to
attract the most attention, but if the simple cases could also be
examined for cost and quality efficiencies, significant improvements might also be discovered. Simple cases tend to be the most
frequent; therefore, small savings in many cases could accumu-
late.

- *Continuing education* is rarely required but potentially beneficial.
Currently, few professional organizations or state licensing
boards require therapists to report continuing education in psychotherapy. The time is rapidly approaching for therapists to
demonstrate that they are continuing to learn (Anderson & Berlant, 1993).

ORGANIZATIONAL STRUCTURES

Psychotherapists are being organized by cost-containing intermediaries into a variety of organizational structures that are intended to
streamline administration and to direct treatment efforts to save money.
They include health maintenance organizations (HMOs), independent
practice associations (IPAs), preferred provider organizations (PPOs),
and point of service (POS).

Originally, HMOs, PPOs, and traditional forms of indemnity insurance were nonoverlapping and distinctly different. (Indemnity insurance protected against loss of health as well as loss of property and
damage to house or car.) Now permutations blur these differences to
create several hybrids that can be placed along a continuum. At one end
lies the freedom of choice and costly indemnity insurance. At the other
end lies highly managed, low-cost, closed panel HMOs. Managed indemnity insurance might have management features including precertification of elective inpatient admissions, with everything else fee-for-
service at the discretion of providers and clients. Closed provider panel
HMOs (closed in that member clients can go only to the psychotherapists on this panel) would tightly control all forms of service and would
include limited pharmacy options and extensive use of group therapy.

In between are a variety of options including preferred provider organizations (PPOs), point of service (POS), and open panel independent practice associations (IPAs) (Wagner, 1993).

HMOs combine the functions of insurer and deliverer of health care, most commonly under a fixed prepaid fee from a payer. Four of the common HMO models are staff model, group practice, network, and IPA, each representing a different way by which the HMO works with providers.

Staff Model

Physicians, therapists, and other providers are directly employed by the HMO and usually are paid by salary, with possible incentives for efficient and effective performance. Also known as "closed panel" HMOs, staff models exclude most community providers except for those with specialties not available in the HMO. These organizations are costly to develop and maintain because of the large fixed salary and benefit expenses for providers and support staff as well as building maintenance and expansion. Because of their need to pay salary and benefits to providers, staff model HMOs are likely to decrease in number, giving way to fee-for-service and capitated risk-sharing models.

Group Model or PSN Model

Rather than support its own staff, a group model HMO contracts with specific groups of providers who are employed by the group practice rather than the HMO. Commonly, the group operates under a capitation rate, but it also can function under a discounted fee-for-service. The discounted fee-for-service is more likely in markets with an excessive number of providers. The high number of providers allows HMOs to reduce the price per unit of service.

This arrangement requires less capital investment by the HMO because it is not responsible for salaries, benefits, or building costs. The group model is disadvantaged because the number of office locations is limited by the number of participating provider group members. Closed panels limit geographical accessibility as well as appearing to constrain provider choice.

Network Model

In the network model, HMOs contract with more than one group practice to provide services. The HMO contracts with several groups for behavioral health or may contract with a primary care group consisting of approximately 10 primary care physicians to provide all-inclusive services. If each primary care group is capitated, then it is responsible for payment to necessary specialists, including psychotherapists, out of its up-front paid capitation rate unless the HMO negotiates rates directly with specialists. The network model provides a wider range of choice for members than the group and staff models.

Individual Practice Association (IPA)

In the IPA model, HMOs contract with an association of providers for member services. Providers belong to a separate legal entity but remain indidual practitioners and retain separate offices and identities. These panels are open to all community physicians who meet the HMO's and IPA's selection criteria. Broad participation of providers ensures that all services will be available, reducing the necessity to refer out of network. Sometimes an HMO forms the IPA with community physicians and therapists, thereby creating its own exclusive provider group.

IPA models require less capital from HMOs to establish and operate. They can provide a broad choice of participating providers who practice in their own offices. Utilization review of IPAs is generally more difficult to manage because providers remain individual practitioners who have little sense for the corporate cost-cutting values required by managed care. As a result, in comparison with costs of the staff and group models, more HMO money may be required for both inpatient and outpatient utilization management.

Preferred Provider Organizations (PPOs)

Preferred provider organizations are preferred therapists under a health benefit plan of employers or of health insurance companies. Providers agree to accept the lower fee-for-service as payment in full except for the applicable copayments. In turn, they are given preference for referrals.

Point of Service (POS)

Point of service plans are hybrids of HMOs and PPOs. POS provides greater consumer choice than the HMO structure but retains its utilization management. Primary care physicians may act as gatekeepers for specialists, but the range of primary care physicians available is greater compared to the HMO panel, and access to specialists is usually easier. Some mature POS plans offer members direct access to mental health services without having to walk past the gatekeeper. Some POS plans reimburse for out-of-network services, but at a significantly lower rate (e.g., 60% for POS instead of 100% for HMO providers). Generally, the monthly premium rate for POS beneficiaries is higher than HMO costs because of the wider range of options offered (Wagner, 1993).

The location of a practice strongly influences the kind of cost-containing organizations one will find.[2] Interestingly, with all these organizational variables, there may not be much difference in the cost-effectiveness between the old indemnity insurance forms and HMO payment schemes.[3]

NOTES

1. Capitation rates are determined by their three basic components: utilization, net cost per unit of service, and profit margin/reserves.

Utilization is described as the compilation of the various units of service (e.g., psychotherapy, pharmacotherapy, hospitalization) per year per thousand employees of the potential purchaser of the plan. An employer provides the MCO with past utilization rates under existing benefit plans for inpatient, outpatient, and other programs. The MCO uses actuarial methods and the company's own experience to forecast costs under the new benefit plan with new coverage provisions.

Net cost per unit of service depends on the MCO's fee schedule, the provider mix (e.g., psychiatrists, PhDs, master's level professionals), the types of services (e.g., partial hospitalization, intensive outpatient, home visits), and applicable copayments and deductibles.

Profit margin is expressed as a percentage of the total premium. The MCO not only tries to build in a reasonable profit margin but also usually tries to develop a reserve to serve as a hedge against unforeseen costs. If the MCO is not able to keep costs under the capitation, it will need additional funds to compensate for the loss.

Rather than simply using employer data, the ideal rate-setting method classifies persons according to their expected costs. For example, a population can be described by a host of demographic variables, including not only age, sex, marital status, socioeconomic status, education level, and urban density but also diet, exercise, personal health histories, family health histories, and exposure to pollution and other environmental toxins. Advanced datasets of the health histories of similar populations modified for variables present in the target population might be used to estimate the health costs of the population; however, no such system currently exists. Rate setters make relatively blind guesses about optimal rates. If revenues and costs for treating specific groups could be closely aligned by an accurate classification system, profits could then be anticipated confidently.

2. Location influences the form of managed care. Managed care takes different forms depending on its environment. Its themes of cost savings through limiting service access, its continuing pressure on providers through utilization review, and its popularity with payers cut across situations.

The HMO penetration of various markets across the country influences the manner in which health care is organized in those markets. If the range of HMO penetration exceeds 25-30%, then HMOs begin to have a major influence on premiums, provider reimbursement, product diversity, and health system organization. HMOs, in 1995, were almost exclusively located in the 561 U.S. metropolitan markets.

Market size also determines the various factors that are necessary for HMOs to grow. In the larger markets, HMO expansion depends on pricing, competition, profit potential, product diversity, HMO enrollment in Medicaid and Medicare, and average length of inpatient stay. The presence of an established HMO industry with high market penetration, favorable lengths of stay, a sizable number of Medicare- or Medicaid-eligible people not yet in HMOs, and lower inpatient days per 1,000 population are some of the factors favoring growth in the larger markets. In the medium-sized markets, HMO enrollment is greatest where a limited number of plans compete using flexible benefits to offer greater choice to payers and consumers. In the smaller markets, HMO enrollment expands when there are fewer HMOs, more unenrolled Medicare and Medicaid clients, and the potential for cost and price efficiency. HMOs increase market penetration and compete for employer business (Kaplan, 1996).

3. The reimbursement system may have little effect on cost-effectiveness. The study described below illustrates the possibility that the payment system may be less important than the service delivery system. Managed care payment scheme variations may be missing the point. Providers may need to find better ways of delivering their care.

This research approach follows tracer conditions through several different systems to measure cost and outcome. The first large-scale study to include depression (or any other serious mental illness) on equal footing with the more commonly studied medical conditions was the Medical Outcome Study (MOS; Wells & Sturm, 1995), a 4-year longitudinal study that started in 1986 and involved more than 20,000 clients in three cities (Boston, Chicago, and Los Angeles). The MOS compared the use of services, quality of care, and health outcomes of adult outpatients with diabetes, hypertension, congestive heart failure, recent myocardial infarction, or depression.

The MOS found no significant differences in functioning outcome between prepaid payment systems and fee-for-service in the treatment of depression; however, prepaid psychiatry and general medical practices showed some evidence of poorer quality of care of depressed clients than their fee-for-service counterparts. Prepaid providers detected depression less often, did less counseling, used more minor tranquilizers, discontinued antidepressants earlier, limited provider continuity, and had somewhat poorer functional outcomes. Fee-for-service, however, was only slightly better despite much higher costs. These findings suggest that the payment system may be less important than the design of more cost-effective delivery systems.

Costs for treatment of depression are lower in general medicine than in psychiatric settings, but outcomes are poorer. Finding the appropriate mix of specialty and general medicine treatment becomes the challenge for system designers who seek sufficient increases in quality with each additional dollar spent.

CHAPTER 2

Mental Health, Inc.

A Fictional Behavioral Health Care Company

Behavioral health care has unique concerns, different from those of primary care and specialty medicine. Separate organizational structures have been developed to manage its requirements. Some therapists saw the future and organized their own companies to respond to the needs of local employers. This chapter describes one such company that has tried to incorporate the tools of cost containment in an effort to develop good quality service while maintaining a profit. It functions in several roles at the same time: as an MCO for companies with which it directly contracts, as the only mental health provider group for an HMO, and as part of an HMO network of providers.

Our hypothetical behavioral care group (based on contributions from B. Hillenberg and F. Yasin) was established in 1988 by Dr. O, a clinical psychologist, and his colleague Dr. I, a psychiatrist. Several principles of partnerships and organization development can be garnered from this case example. First, the partners had to trust each other. Second, they had to find a way to distribute their talents and interests effectively. Third, they needed to establish clear guidelines for the conduct of employees in their organization; for example, they recognized that therapists (not only psychiatrists) had to carry beepers and be re-sponsible for emergencies. They also recognized that healthy, happy, and rested employees are more cost-effective.

Drs. I and O had met at a cocktail party in the home of Mr. B, a prominent businessman in their city of 500,000. Mr. B wanted to find a way to cut mental health costs for various businesses, as he had done with general medical costs. Mr. B had developed several contracts with local corporations to handle health insurance needs for their employ-ees. He had shown a promising reduction in the rate of increase in the health care expenditures of these corporations by finding physician groups willing to accept discounted fee-for-service, precertification be-fore hospitalization, and prior authorization before major laboratory evaluations. In return, these clinicians received an increased volume of patient referrals. Mr. B did not see, however, a corresponding drop in mental health services costs. Because Mr. B thought Dr. I and Dr. O might enjoy working together, he invited them to his party and made his proposal to them. With the usual caution of mental health profes-sionals, they agreed to discuss it further.

Out of these discussions emerged the foundation of Mental Health, Inc., a behavioral health network. The legal and planning work as well as initial capital investments were provided by Mr. B. The network con-sisted of clinic office buildings located in the four corners of the city. Each clinic office was within 30 minutes of an inpatient psychiatric unit with which contracts were arranged. Fortunately for Drs. I and O, they walked into a situation in which they immediately had the opportunity to provide mental health services for 25,000 clients. Unfortunately, they had to scramble to find providers who were willing to continuously adapt to their evolving system. They were in for a bumpy but profitable ride.

The first major area of cost savings was provided by careful utiliza-tion review of inpatient services, both before admission and during hospitalization. They quickly recognized the need for a full continuum of care; they set up day treatment and intensive outpatient services. They also connected themselves to the powerful self-help movement taking root in their city and were delighted to discover that a directory for self-help groups had been developed with the support of state fund-ing. In addition, the state Department of Mental Health and the self-help groups themselves were providing sufficient financial support both to create and maintain a 1-800 number to answer questions about these groups and to print and mail brochures describing the available groups.

As Drs. I and O worked together, they discovered that their talents and interests were different and complementary. Dr. I loved clinical work and enjoyed trying to make it more efficient and cost-effective. Dr. O loved to talk with people, have long lunches, throw parties, and wine and dine prospective contractees. He liked talking about clinical work more than doing it. Dr. I became "Mr. Inside," working on cost-effective clinical care and quality improvement, while Dr. O became "Mr. Outside," making the contracts and dealing with lawyers, the MCOs, hospital administrations, and personnel issues. Dr. I took the title of Medical Director, and Dr. O took the title of Administrator.

They assembled a staff of professionals with various backgrounds, allowing each profession to determine the range of activities within its realm. At first, they paid the staff a salary with benefits, but they discovered that many of the staff found ways to pass work off to others. They changed the salary to a percentage of the fee collected, based on a discounted fee-for-service scale they had established for their own organization when they assumed risk through capitation. Psychiatrists received the highest percentage, PhD psychologists the next highest, and master's level professionals the lowest. They found that non-MDs preferred to allow the psychiatrists to take all after-hours calls, and that this policy was creating a high turnover among psychiatrists. They convinced the therapists to carry beepers for their own clients, leaving only the most severe crisis situations for psychiatric input. After instituting this policy, psychiatrists remained on staff much longer on average.

Because psychiatrists cost more than other providers, they were restricted to doing what they are uniquely trained to do: make diagnoses and offer medications. Contrary to expectations, however, two psychiatrists in the group showed that they could be cost-effective in doing both psychotherapy (for shorter sessions than the standard 50-minute hour) and pharmacotherapy. Some clients noted on their satisfaction surveys that they appreciated having one provider for both treatments. The network's information system, which collected data on quality and cost, provided the opportunity to discover this somewhat unexpected result. The reason these psychiatrists could be more cost-effective was their efficient use of time. Each saw psychotherapy clients for 20-40 minutes rather than 50 minutes, and each dictated notes quickly so that no more than 1-3 minutes passed between visits. The traditional therapy hour provides a 10-minute break between clients, an inefficient use of time. The staff speculated that there was also a built-in efficiency in having one person do both treatments because only one strong working alliance was required.

PhD psychologists saw the more difficult psychotherapy clients and supervised master's level therapist/counselors (at an hourly rate paid by Mental Health, Inc.) for work with their more difficult clients. A psychiatric nurse did both psychotherapy and pharmacotherapy for some of the clients stabilized on maintenance medications.

One of the master's level psychotherapists preferred the triage function, helping clients find the most appropriate provider. In this area, continuing quality improvement became an enjoyable challenge for everyone. Psychotherapy research has not answered the client-therapist matching question very well; thus, the triage worker and staff members were charting unknown territory. One difficult triage consideration is matching the type of presenting problem to the appropriate therapist. In this case, one therapist liked to see borderline clients, despite the additional problems created by managed care limits on session numbers. Others liked anxiety disorders, depression, women's issues, and eating disorders. Any client with depression, anxiety, psychotic disorders, borderline personality, or bipolar disorder, however, had to be referred for psychiatric evaluation after the first psychotherapy session; otherwise, the therapist was not paid for subsequent sessions. This policy was instituted in response to several therapists who believed that their therapeutic skills were sufficient to manage any depression or anxiety disorder. The company believed that this was a misjudgment that often led to extra therapy sessions. This decision was based on clinical impressions, not clinical research.

The triage worker also took client preference for certain therapist characteristics into consideration, recognizing that a positive working alliance improves outcome (Horvath & Greenberg, 1994). Some clients preferred a male or female therapist; others wanted a therapist with a specific religious orientation. Language and ethnic variables also were considered. The company, however, would not tolerate discrimination by clients against the one African American psychiatrist. If a complaint was registered because of race, the company reported the client to the managed care company handling the plan or directly to the payer.

The company offered a full continuum of care for child, adolescent, adult, and geriatric clients for the following problem areas:

- Chemical dependency

- Eating disorders

- Posttraumatic stress disorder (PTSD)

- Attention Deficit Hyperactive Disorder (ADHD)

- Women's issues

For chronically distressed clients including those who are border-line, chronic depressive, schizophrenic, or have bipolar disorders, they offered groups. Copayments increased after more than 20 therapy sessions within a year.

Both Dr. I and Dr. O wanted their system to be considerate of their therapists, recognizing that providers are under continual pressure to improve the quality and cost-effectiveness of their care. Tired workers are not cost-effective. For example, a tired utilization reviewer is apt to say "yes" more often than "no" to a precertification for hospitalization request, because denial takes more energy than approval. They insisted that therapists define a personal upper limit to therapy hours to prevent burnout. Some were effective at 36 hours per week, whereas others managed better at 22. They also tried to prevent confusion about psychotropic medications. Dr. I insisted that the psychiatrists use standard drugs with which the therapists could become familiar so that they could more easily recognize the side effects requiring more immediate psychiatric consultation. For example, all therapists knew that for clients taking Haldol, a report of a feeling of "not being able to sit still" could lead to the client stopping the medication.

The earlier a problem is addressed, the less likely it is to escalate into something catastrophic and costly. The company therefore placed a great deal of importance on accessibility. Its clinicians developed a system for crisis and urgent appointments and were readily available during evening office hours and weekends, especially for Saturday morning appointments.

Dr. I began to thrive in this challenging, varied environment. He loved to drive to the four business offices to review charts, hunting for treatment decisions that might impede recovery. He noticed that some psychiatrists underprescribed neuroleptics, fearing side effects including tardive dyskinesia. He noted that some therapists failed to enlist the aid of spouses who could help monitor the affective swings of clients with manic-depressive illness. Early detection of mania or depression could prevent hospitalization and reduce costs. These and other quality indicators increasingly became part of the therapeutic culture. Drs. I and O believed that good client care reduces costs. They collected evidence that began to substantiate this belief.

One of the more troublesome aspects of their operation was managing grievances. They could not predict clients' complaints. Perhaps the lights were too bright, or the carpet too dirty, or someone did not like the magazines in the waiting room or the fact that it had no windows. Some clients realized that Mental Health, Inc. was their only alternative for mental health treatment. They believed that they were Mental Health, Inc. prisoners, so they complained. Some clients did not like the therapist to whom they were assigned and requested another one. For borderline clients and some chemical dependency clients, the Mental Health, Inc. rules against changing therapists created much consternation. Mental Health, Inc. allowed only one switch. If someone left the hospital or other treatment program against the advice of a psychiatrist or therapist, no further services were provided until a third party (the HMO or payer) resolved the dispute.

Mental Health, Inc. had different contracts with different organizations, sometimes functioning under capitation, other times under discounted fee-for-service. Sometimes clients could come directly to Mental Health, Inc. without going through a gatekeeper; other arrangements required that a primary care physician act as gatekeeper.

One of the contracts stipulated that no client could receive more than 20 mental health visits. A mental health visit was defined as any visit to a mental health practitioner, whether psychiatrist, psychologist, or master's level therapist, each of whom was paid on a fee-for-service basis. Mental Health, Inc. made more money when the client was seen by a master's level therapist because the margin between what they were paid and what the master's level person cost was greater than that for PhDs and MDs or DOs (doctors of osteopathy). Under this contract, therefore, Mental Health, Inc. preferred to have master's level therapists see clients rather than psychiatrists or PhD psychologists. If the primary care physician provided medications, this visit was not counted as a mental health visit. The administrators therefore developed several methods to support primary care physicians (PCP) prescribing medications, including a telephone number to receive direct consultation from Mental Health, Inc. psychiatrists. In addition, the company devised and distributed a newsletter describing the newest developments in psychopharmacology to the primary care physicians in this plan. Successful pharmacotherapy by the PCP permitted more sessions for the master's level therapists, better client care, and more profit.

The Mental Health, Inc. providers became sensitive to which kinds of clients the PCPs would manage. These were clients with no comorbid Axis I diagnosis, strong family and social support, and stable lifestyles. PCPs were not willing to manage clients with multiple Axis I diagnoses, those with personality disorders, and those with no social and family support who led unstable work and social lives, were highly emotional, and were prone to crisis. These clients were seen by the psychiatrists.

As the number of behavioral health care competitors decreases as a result of mergers and acquisitions, what of the future of Mental Health, Inc.? In 1995, 11 companies controlled 89% of the managed behavioral health market, with 60% of privately insured people enrolled in managed care plans (Hutchins, 1995b, quoting Diane Rush Woods). Perhaps if Mental Health, Inc. were a real company, it would have been purchased already by one of these behavioral health care giants.

CHAPTER 3

Payers, Providers, and the Evolution of Managed Care

Therapists want to survive and thrive economically. Payers want to pay less and receive more. The laws of supply and demand, of buying and selling, have taken hold. Payers and their MCOs are becoming more and more like management. Providers are becoming more and more like laborers in a factory who may either join management, create their own businesses, or remain on the behavioral health assembly line. This chapter describes these two opposing camps in the context of the evolution of managed care.

BUSINESSES AND GOVERNMENT SEEK COST CONTAINMENT

To demonstrate the anxiety facing health care payers, consider the following: In 1985, health care expenditures absorbed 10% of the gross domestic product (GDP). By 1994, they accounted for 14% of the GDP (Fox, 1995; Levit, Lazenby, & Sivarajan, 1996). Per capita health care expenditures rose from $1,700 per person in 1985 to $3,500 in 1994 (Levit et al., 1996).

Projected health care expenditures are even more sobering as we anticipate an increasingly large and older population. In 1995, U.S. national health care costs reached $1 trillion. By 2030, the projected annual expenditure for health care will reach $16 trillion (Health Care Financing Administration, 1996). (At a 3% inflation rate for 35 years, $1 trillion dollars would equal $2.8 trillion dollars; therefore, the inflation-adjusted cost for health expenditures in 2030 are estimated to be more than five times mid-1990s costs.)

Payers can no longer afford these rapidly increasing costs. The only apparent alternative proposal to the current market economy approach—a single-payer system—was defeated by Congress during the early years of the Clinton administration. Cost containment has been left to the market forces of capitalism that were vigorously introduced to the world with the Industrial Revolution, begun in 18th century England.

Health care is being industrialized. Health care has gone from a cottage industry of small and medium-size practitioner groups to corporate management with greater attention to cost savings and demands for continued increases in productivity, examined by using discrete and measurable outcomes. This dramatic change follows as another wave of the Industrial Revolution that began when individual makers of clothing and other goods were replaced by factory workers on assembly lines tending machines powered by steam engines. Individual producers of consumer goods were replaced by technologically advanced, highly organized teams of laborers, resulting in significant social and economic turmoil. Greater efficiency puts people out of work: individual shoemakers lost their buyers to lower priced, machine-made products; telephone operators were replaced by computerized switchboards; and car wash workers were replaced by mechanical hoses and brushes. Medical visits are being transformed into commodities. Job displacement and loss are taking place as less expensive workers replace those who were paid more. Looking at the broad context within which these changes are taking place will help us to understand more clearly what is happening and how to respond.

The essential forces behind the Industrial Revolution were (a) increased sources of power through technological innovation beginning with the steam engine and (b) increased scale in worker organization that facilitated specialization and coordination of production beginning with the factory (Stearns, 1993). The Industrial Revolution rendered many skills obsolete and made workers dependent on fluctuating market forces. People felt they had less control over their destinies as machines took over their responsibilities. Workers were known to attack machines in blind fury over their lack of control over working conditions, much as some therapists vent their anger at managed care caseworkers. Workers could be fired for revolting, their houses and their livelihoods taken from them by factory owners. Similarly, angry psychotherapists have been dropped from provider panels for protesting too much.

Life expectancy in Britain increased, however, during the Industrial Revolution, and markets expanded as consumer goods became more readily available (Stearns, 1993). Perhaps this historical fact implies some potential benefits to the mental health economic revolution. Governments supported industrialization by providing essential education and technological research, which benefited workers, but they also expanded police forces to keep rebellious workers in line, suggesting the potential for both positive and negative effects. Eventually, governments began to regulate industrial excesses such as child labor exploitation and environmental pollution (Stearns, 1993). Exploitation of the sick through denial of care is to be addressed by both state and federal legislation. Pollution by managed care companies is represented by the contamination of the doctor-client relationship through breaches of confidentiality, interference in delivering optimal care, and major distortions in the psychotherapy process.

In health care delivery systems, the two essential innovations of this revolution are, as in previous reforms, technological and organizational. The technological innovations are represented by tremendous increases in the medical knowledge base. Known as clinical pathway algorithms or decision trees, these are sequential guidelines for treating specific problems. These decision trees are aiding and in some cases replacing clinician experience and intuition. More than 100 well-accepted clinical pathways exist for medical problems including breast cancer, diabetes, hip fractures, stroke, and idiopathic thrombocytopenia (Vibbert & Youngs, 1995).

The organizational innovations in mental health delivery were described in Chapter 1. Like shoemakers who moved from their own cottages to factory assembly lines, psychotherapists are being held to uniform standards imposed by bureaucratic hierarchies as a means of increasing efficiency and providing profit for management. Whether these technological and organizational innovations actually *improve* mental health and medical care has yet to be demonstrated (see note 3, Chapter 1).

THE MAJOR PAYER GROUPS

Payers, rather than the MCOs, are the central force in the shift toward managing health care. MCOs are fulfilling the desire of the major payers to reduce their health care costs and reap their profits. (The profit motive of MCOs adds yet another financial squeeze on therapists.)

Before managed care, most financial risk was held by insurance companies and by large self-insured employers. If total costs for a specific population exceeded the insurance premiums paid by employers and employees, the insurance company or the self-insured business was required to make up the difference. In other words, the insurance company or the business was at risk. At policy renewal time, the insurance company would project future costs and manage future risk by either increasing the premium or, in some cases, not renewing the policy. There was little incentive to control costs as long as the employers (and employees) were willing to pay ever-increasing premiums (Mauer, Jarvis, Mockler, & Trabin, 1995). The insurance companies benefited from increased premiums because they took a fixed percentage from the incoming premium revenue stream: The larger the stream, the larger the total income to the insurance company.

In 1995, mental health expenditures in the United States were distributed as follows: 40% of health care expenditures came from private insurance (including managed care) and from individual clients; 22% came from the federal government through Medicare, Medicaid, the Department of Veterans Affairs, and other programs; and spending by state and local governments accounted for the other 38% (Iglehart, 1996). Under the old indemnity insurance plans, therapists could collect from individual insurance policies. Now, as payers flex their market muscle, practitioners must understand their needs and idiosyncrasies in orders to be paid. These major payers include employers, Medicare, Medicaid, CHAMPUS, prison systems, and the uninsured.

Table 3.1   Number of Employees and Percentage With
Group Health Plans

Type of Occupation	Number (millions)	Percentage
Executive, administrative, managerial	17	68
Professional, specialty	18	67
Technical/related support	4	67
Sales workers	17	41
Administrative support including clerical	21	57
Precision production, craft, repair	15	56
Machine operators, assemblers	8	60
Transportation, material moving	6	57
Handlers, equipment cleaners	6	36
Service worker	21	30
Farming, forestry, and fishing	4	20
Armed forces	1	25
Total	137	52

SOURCE: *The American Almanac 1995-1996* (1996).

NOTE: Armed forces stationed on military bases have their medical care provided by other military personnel on the base and therefore are not considered to be in a plan.

Employers

In 1993, approximately 137 million Americans were employed. Approximately 50% of the employed were covered by a group health plan. Table 3.1 shows a breakdown of occupational status and the percentage of each group covered by a group health plan. Knowledge of these employees can help health care providers target their services.

Both large and small employer groups want rapid response, quick results, low costs, and continuing employee functioning. They want employees to be satisfied with their health care assistance. Large multisite businesses want regional or countrywide delivery systems, whereas small businesses are likely to form local cooperatives to purchase health care at a group discount.

Medicare

Medicare is a federal program developed primarily for older and disabled adults. Medicare provided health care coverage for 37 million

Americans in 1994. The distribution of benefits among enrollees was skewed: An estimated 11% accounted for 73% of payments (again demonstrating the 20/80 rule of utilization suggesting that 20% of the people use 80% of the resources). In 1994, Medicare spent $166 billion on services including hospital care, physician and other professional services, home health care, and nursing homes (Burner & Waldo, 1995).

Medicare, begun in the mid-1960s, is facing severe financial problems as the overall population ages and there are relatively fewer active workers paying into the system. Medicare Part A covers hospital expenses and is paid for by a 2.9% payroll tax. Medicare Part B covers physicians' bills; 31% of its funding comes directly from Medicare enrollees and 69% from general tax revenues. When enacted, Part A was self-sufficient, financed solely by the payroll taxes. Unfortunately, this self-sufficiency has not been maintained. Hospital costs now exceed by three times individual payroll tax contributions; therefore, when an enrollee enters the hospital, current expenses are met only one-third from the individual's contribution, with the remaining two-thirds paid by payroll taxes on current workers' income. Some estimates show Part A running a deficit by the year 2001 or earlier unless cost-saving legislation is enacted.

Baby boomers (born between 1946 and 1952) will begin reaching age 65 in 2011. Over the next decade, while the overall population increases by about 2%, the retired population will increase nearly 30%. In a single decade, the ratio of workers to retired will go from the current 5:1 to 3:1. Workers will no longer be able to support the current beneficiaries or be able to reap the benefit of their contributions (Hood, 1996). The baby boom cohort is better educated and more demanding of excellent health care than the current retirees. They are likely to live longer and will demand more of the expensive treatments that technology will make available. As their concerns for their own health grow, they are likely to vote to reduce outlays for defense, foreign aid, and education while increasing tax expenditures on health care programs (Raspberry, 1996).

Efforts to reduce Medicare costs are likely to include the curbing of fraud, abuse, and waste. Payroll taxes likely will be increased. Beneficiaries are likely to be asked to carry higher costs. Clients will be encouraged to join managed care plans, and provider and hospital payments are likely to be capped.

Medicaid

A state-federal program varying by state, Medicaid is designed to serve three separate populations. Medicaid spending is as follows: 70% goes to nursing homes for the care of indigent, primarily older people; 15% goes to Transitional Assistance to Needy Families (TANF) for both medical and mental health problems of children and pregnant mothers, children in state custody, and refugees; and 15% goes to the severely and persistently mentally ill and other disabled people.

In 1994, 35 million people received some type of Medicaid benefit. Children and adults in families with dependent children represented 71% of the recipients yet consumed only 28% of the program payments. The aged, blind, and disabled represented about 25% of the recipients but consumed almost 75% of the payments. In 1994, Medicaid spent $34 billion, largely for inpatient services, including hospital and nursing home care. For at least two decades, Medicaid has funded about 50% of nursing home costs (Health Care Financing Administration, 1996).

Much tighter controls on Medicaid are likely. Possibilities include

- Elimination of guaranteed Medicaid eligibility for all non-elderly disabled Social Security Insurance (SSI) beneficiaries. For example, some substance abusers and children diagnosed with serious psychiatric disorders may not be deemed deserving of this coverage, and/or wealthier recipients may be cut from the program.

- Omission of federal oversight of Medicaid programs. States could design programs as they wish.

- States could be allowed to reduce the mandated contributions to their Medicaid programs and also be permitted to create locked-in managed care programs that do not allow consumer choice of another plan (Finley, 1996).

Civilian Health and Medical Program of the Uniformed Services (CHAMPUS)

CHAMPUS is an entitlement health care program administered by the Department of Defense that pays for care delivered by civilian health providers to retirees and to the dependents of active duty members and retirees. The uniformed services include the Army, Navy, Air Force, Marine Corps, Commissioned Corps of the Public Health Service, Coast Guard, and National Oceanic and Atmospheric Administration. Fiscal intermediaries administer the program, which requires the dependents of active duty members to share outpatient costs and requires retirees and their dependents to share both outpatient and inpatient costs. In 1996, 5 million people were eligible for CHAMPUS (Morgan, Morgan, & Quinto, 1996). The Department of Defense has instituted a managed care alternative to CHAMPUS called TRICARE as part of its effort to reduce costs.

Prison System

The prison system contains a disproportionately high percentage of people with mental illness and substance abuse. In 1992, 850,000 adults were in state or federal prisons serving maximum sentences of at least 1 year. Of these, 804,000 were male and 46,000 were female; 412,000 were white and 428,000 were black. In 1970, 200,000 adults were in prison at a rate of 97 per 100,000 population. In 1994, 910,000 adults were imprisoned in state or federal institutions at a rate of 353 per 100,000 adults (*The American Almanac 1995-1996*, 1996). As the United States continues to imprison a relatively high percentage of its citizens compared to other nations, the need for mental health services in prisons is likely to expand.

Uninsured

Between 1991 and 1993, one-third of adults 18-64 years old (about 35 million) were uninsured for some period of time, with 18% uninsured at any one point in time. In 1993, half of the unemployed, 45% of part-time workers, 35% of students, and 27% of full-time workers had been uninsured for some period during the previous 2 years. Half had been uninsured for more than 1 year. Almost one million people, or 3% of the uninsured, could not obtain insurance because of poor health, illness, or age. One-third of the uninsured reported that they did not receive needed health care, compared to 9% of the insured. The uninsured group remains a major health policy problem. Forgoing needed care can affect both health status and cost of eventual care (Davis, Rowland, Altman, Collins, Morris, 1995).

These payer groups, including some of the uninsured who could pay on their own, are the targets for MCO marketing strategies and contract competition. They and their administrative agents decide the nature of benefit plans and the panels of providers. They are the movers behind the managed care revolution. The payer groups seek cost containment.

HEALTH CARE PROFESSIONALS
SEEK PROFIT TOO

The health care system of the past was composed of a remarkable collection of independent hospital clinics, solo practitioners, and small professional groups. Each passed along its costs to a wide variety of public and private insurance companies who turned their costs back to employers, consumers, and the public. Professional self-interest fostered legislation that reduced competition and expanded domain. Like other businesspeople, physicians and psychotherapy professionals sought ways to maximize profit. Physician entrepreneurs developed medical diagnostic laboratories (e.g., for blood tests and X rays) to which they referred clients and from which they received a percentage of the cash flow. Subsequent legislation reduced this practice, but the clever few still find ways around such restrictions.

Good evidence suggests that often unwarranted expansion of mental health services took place in the 1980s. During this time, profit-making inpatient drug and alcohol services and adolescent psychiatric programs grew exponentially. Data supporting these approaches did not provide the driving force behind this expansion; rather, it was benefit packages that uncritically provided for 28-day substance abuse treatment programs and long inpatient child and adolescent stays (Boyle & Callahan, 1995). The freedom to make extra money through liberal benefit plans has come to an end.

THE HEALTH CARE WORKFORCE

This section describes an important context for therapists—the various influences on the health care workforce supply. Psychotherapists are

Table 3.2   Factors Influencing the Number of Health Care Workers

Reimbursement policies of major payers
- Federal government
- State government
- Business

Professional policies

Educational institution policies

one of many groups who contribute to the health of Americans. The forces affecting the status of other health care workers also influence the functional status of psychotherapists. The key fact about other health care workers is, as evidence suggests, that the health care workforce supply is too large.[1]

In the absence of a national health care policy, a patchwork of influences has determined the supply of the health care workforce. Table 3.2 summarizes these influences.

The numbers of health care workers are determined by *need* and *demand*. Need is an epidemiologically based measure of the amount of services necessary to keep a given population healthy. Demand measures a population's willingness to utilize (and often to pay for) health care services. There are no commonly agreed upon means to determine these measures, yet need and demand strongly influence the supply of professionals.

The major influence on demand is *reimbursement policy* of the major payers in health care, including the federal government, state governments, and business. The professions themselves influence supply, as do their educational institutions. Reimbursement strategies were once designed to improve access to care; now, reimbursement strategies are being designed to reduce demand and therefore supply. Following is a summary of these often competing influences on workforce supply.

At the federal level, Medicare, Medicaid, and other social insurance policies have provided increased access to third-party coverage for health services. Indirect supply policies such as Medicare payments for graduate medical and nursing training have also increased supply. In addition, direct policy interventions such as student assistance, training grants, construction grants, and other support to teaching institutions also have increased workforce numbers.

At the state level, Medicaid policies also increased access to third-party payers and to health care. State governments have actively increased supply through direct financial support of universities, community colleges, area health education centers, research facilities, and teaching hospitals.

The marketplace has had its own effects. Insurance companies have greatly influenced the type and character of the health professions and their training by focusing on reimbursement for procedures, diagnostic testing, and inpatient hospitalizations while being unwilling to provide coverage for primary care and preventive care (Osterweis & McLaughlin, 1995). The gradual agreement by insurance companies to fund psychotherapy provided by nonpsychiatrists fostered the development and proliferation of schools of professional psychology and other nonacademic psychotherapy training programs. More schools of social work began to specialize in psychotherapy training, as did academic programs in educational psychology.

As hospital lengths of stay are reduced, the demand for hospital-based nurses is reduced. The emphasis on primary care dramatically increases the demand for advanced practice nurses in outpatient settings. As managed care companies reduce the provider-to-population ratios, they are also changing the mix of physicians to nonphysicians. This saves money but does not necessarily provide equivalent or better outcomes. Some managed care companies, fearing that academic institutions are not properly training their students in managed care principles, have established their own residency training programs for family practice. Some are considering starting their own medical schools (Osterweis & McLaughlin, 1995).

The *health professions*, primarily through professional associations, have influenced workforce supply directly by controlling state credentialing processes. By limiting the number of practitioners, professional organizations have tried to decrease competition and therefore stabilize fees. Dentistry, for example, has successfully encouraged or perpetuated licensure legislation that limits state supplies of dentists.

Educational institutions influence supply by deciding the type, character, and size of their professional programs and schools. Funding lines strongly influence such decisions. At one time, the federal government encouraged the growth of specialized, hospital-based physicians. More recently, incentives have been turned toward increasing the number of primary care physicians and reducing the number of specialists.

Research supported by federal or private sources influences demand by creating new medications, devices, and procedures that create new types of specialty health providers, including numerous allied health personnel such as cytologists, x-ray technologists, perfusionists, and genetic counselors. For example, research findings in cognitive therapy for depression showed its equivalence to an antidepressant (Rush, Beck, Kovacs, & Hollon, 1977) and thus strongly increased the demand for this form of psychotherapy. Research can and should reduce the need for providers by producing more efficient means for treatment and prevention (Osterweis & McLaughlin, 1995).

Workforce Supply Projections

The Pew Health Professions Commission (1995) observed that we have been operating under a supply- rather than demand-driven workforce in which more professionals meant the creation of more jobs. That is no longer true. Providers are now being asked to respond to the needs of populations. This observation led the commission to the following predictions:

1. There will be closure of half the nation's hospitals and elimination of 60% of hospital beds.
2. There will be a surplus of 100,000 to 150,000 physicians as the demand for specialty care shrinks and primary care expands, a surplus of 200,000 to 300,000 nurses generated by hospital closings, and a surplus of 40,000 pharmacists as the dispensing function for drugs is automated and centralized.
3. There will be a fundamental alteration of the health professional schools and the ways they organize, structure, and frame their programs of education, research, and client care.

In 1997, the Health Care Financing Administration closed an agreement with 41 teaching hospitals in New York State to reduce the number of residents being trained there. For $700,000,000 over 7 years, the schools agreed to significant reductions in resident numbers. The money paid to them would be gradually reduced each year as the hospitals found other ways to meet the service demands previously handled by the residents. To illustrate this trend, consider that in mental health between 1989 and 1992, 30% of private sector mental health treatment providers (mostly inpatient facilities) went out of business (Hutchins, 1995b).

Psychotherapists need to address the policy questions that define the purpose of psychotherapy in American society and from which workforce training and distribution is planned. The supply of psycho-therapists will be strongly affected by the goals of the health structure within which therapists function. For example, if future health policy strongly advocates the value and usefulness of mental health in pro-moting physical well-being, then there will be a crucial role for psycho-therapists in the future health care system. If future health policy rejects the value of psychotherapy, then psychotherapy will begin to disap-pear.

THE EVOLUTION OF MANAGED CARE: MANAGING COSTS, CARE, OR HEALTH?

Three phases of managed care seem to be operating at the same time across different systems, directed by different employers and different managed care organizations. Some MCOs want only short-term finan-cial gain, hoping to make big profits and sell out to the highest bidder. Others want to establish a long-term presence in particular market-places. These different business goals influence the forms managed care takes. Some manage costs by denying access, some manage care by im-proving therapist efficiency, and some manage health through preven-tion and early intervention. These three approaches form a rough out-line of the stages through which managed care systems evolve. Therapists have a different role under each management objective.

Systems that simply *manage costs* use a variety of mechanisms to limit access to clinicians and to limit coverage, and thereby to reduce payments. The early phase of managing costs emphasized discounts from established charges, utilization review, and second opinions (for major procedures like surgery). How did providers respond? They in-creased rates every year to make up for the discount. For example, if in year 1 my established fee is $80 and I agree to receive $60, then the next year I establish my fee at $100 and collect $75. The following year, I might raise my fee to $120 to collect $90. In this way, the discounted fee begins to catch up with the fee that I might have received had I not agreed to the discount.

Mechanisms to control costs more tightly were developed in response. These include gatekeepers to behavioral health, excluding coverage for specific disorders (e.g., chronic schizophrenia), high client copayments at the time of service, offering providers located far away (some clients must travel several hours to see the psychiatrist approved for their plan), and annual maximum benefit limitations (on inpatient days, dollars, and visits).

Short-term profits can soar when access is restricted through excluding people with chronic illnesses or genetic predispositions to major diseases; by limiting length and type of treatment; by using less expensive, nonphysician mental health professionals; and by strictly defining medical necessity (for treatment). If only the healthy are covered and the sick are excluded, profits are maximized. An additional profit raiser requires that providers be paid by a discounted fee-for-service. Initial evaluations and therapy sessions are reimbursed at lower and lower rates. The guarantee of reimbursement makes up for some of the loss from uncollected billings from clients who fail to pay.

To grasp the profit potential from mental health management, consider the following example. The per member per month (pmpm) costs of unmanaged care are around $8. An MCO is willing to manage care for $5 pmpm in the first 2 years. Actually, they can do it for $2.50 by denying access, so the MCO makes a big profit: $2.50 pmpm = $30 per member per year of profit. With 20,000 covered lives, the MCO grosses $600,000 per year above treatment costs. If the administrative cost is 10% of the total premium, then administrative costs (10% × $5 pmpm × 12 × 20,000 lives) = $120,000. Net Profit = $600,000 − $120,000 = $480,000. The percentage profit is $480,000/$1,200,000 = 40%. In other words, 40% of the premium becomes profit for the MCO.

Some MCOs *manage care* by carefully monitoring outcomes according to strict standards in their health care delivery systems. Some of these management mechanisms include decredentialing ineffective providers, protocols for treatment planning, and continuing quality improvement to yield greater efficiency and cost-effectiveness. MCO case managers begin to disappear as therapists adopt managed care principles without external oversight (including becoming sensitive to the cost of each service rendered and to limited financial resources, to the needs of the general population being served rather than individual clients, and to the value of seeking out system efficiencies and inefficiencies). The disappearance of intermediaries will reduce MCO overhead and possibly permit increases in amounts paid to therapists. Managed care companies may become consultants to groups that will manage themselves.

More advanced managed care systems *manage health* by helping enrollees stay healthy. Mechanisms for managing health include education programs, outreach to high utilizers, self-help groups, wellness programs, newsletters about health maintenance, and illness prevention. In the future, prospective clients may be able to use the Internet to access Web pages that will help them to self-diagnose and treat as a means of catching disease processes early in their course. Nurses may use computerized algorithms to make diagnoses before patients are seen by physicians, if they need to be seen at all. Clients may find computerized therapy programs before being seen by a psychotherapist.

When managing health, providers strive to keep people well by emphasizing prevention and health-promoting practices. They are paid by the up-front capitation contracts to reduce health care visits. For example, large-group couple interventions for marital enhancement might be shown to prevent divorce and its consequent effects on spouses and children. When people become sick, providers strive to treat them in the most cost-effective way. The overall health of the population being served becomes the primary outcome measure. Managers of health care systems carefully determine the appropriate team mix for a population—the number of psychiatrists, PhD psychologists, and social workers. Auxiliary aids are strongly emphasized, including Alcoholics Anonymous, sex abuse groups, self-help books (some are written and sold by clinic staff), group therapy, encouragement of the development of self-help groups, and Internet chat groups.

Advanced systems may incorporate the burgeoning knowledge of mind-body interaction and capitalize on its growing popularity. Some are already advocating systematic recommendations for a healthy life including careful dietary regulation emphasizing vegetarian cooking, reasonable dietary supplements, consistent exercise, and minimal medical interventions for relatively minor disorders (Weil, 1995). Perhaps we will see that psychotherapists will be trained to be models of mental and physical well-being.

Prevention programs resemble existing efforts to inoculate and immunize against disease. Keyboard operators are shown how to avoid carpal tunnel syndrome. People who lift heavy weights are shown how to avoid back injuries. Programs are being developed for early intervention with children who are at risk for depression (Seligman, 1995). Parents with histories of depression are taught to help their children confront and overcome the biochemical and role-model-induced depression behaviors of learned helplessness and apathy.

Psychotherapists can judge whether their managed care system is managing costs (most of them are), managing care, or managing the health of their capitated population. As these systems evolve, therapists can better predict and develop their roles in these new contexts.

The industrialization of mental health care and rush toward cost containment have challenged the ethics of psychotherapeutic practice. The next chapter addresses these painful distortions in the hopes of redressing them.

NOTE

1. In 1985, the number of persons employed at health service sites was 7.9 million. In 1993, the number had grown to 10.5 million, an increase of more than 2.5 million (National Center for Health Statistics, 1995). More had seemed better until recently. In 1985, the total number of active physicians was 497,000. Eight years later, nearly another 100,000 had been added, to total 591,000 (National Center for Health Statistics, 1995).

Since 1965, most of the growth in physicians per capita in the United States has been in the specialties, with the number per 100,000 population rising from 56 in 1965 to 123 in 1992. Over the same period, by contrast, the number of generalists per 100,000 population increased only slightly from 59 to 67, and the proportion of physicians in generalist practice fell from 51% to 35% (Kindig, 1995).

THE CLASH BETWEEN COST CONTAINMENT AND CLIENT CARE

Cost containment is twisting psychotherapists' practice in once un-imaginable ways. The freedom to do well by doing good in the spirit of American free enterprise is vanishing from the mental health treatment landscape. Instead, therapists are now wrestling with daunting challenges described in the first section, but also with understanding the major ethical and treatment questions erected by these organizational-economic forces. Chapter 4 insists that therapists examine the moral intent of health care insurance and come to some conclusions regarding this contentious issue. Intrusions by overseers clearly alter confidentiality. How do you intend to respond to them? Even more threatening to therapists' relationship with clients is the tension between the role as an agent of cost containment and the role as a client advocate. The more a therapist advocates for a client, the more money the client costs, and the less "valuable" the therapist is to the MCO. The chapter concludes with a long-standing question: Should one do what is best for each individual or offer the greatest good to the greatest number by spreading out limited resources?

Therapists are understandably frightened and angry about these new influences. The once predictable future has disappeared, replaced by economic uncertainty and demands to conduct psychotherapy to contain costs. As described in Chapter 5, therapists are learning new self-instructions and adapting to shifts in the stages of the psychotherapeutic process.

The next generations of psychotherapists will experience the greatest uncertainty of all. Attracted to this marvelous helping profession by its many appeals, as were their predecessors, they require much more help to become economically viable practitioners. Training programs must heed the call for fast, decisive transformation to fulfill the need for outcome-based, efficient, and effective psychotherapy education that mirrors the demands of the cost-containment marketplace.

CHAPTER 4

Ethics of Client Care Under Cost Containment

The cost-containment motive is reshaping the contract between pro-viders and clients. The impulse to contain costs establishes impediments to effective client care. This chapter reviews four major ethical dilemmas created by this clash between the profit motive and clinical care: (a) the moral intent of health insurance, (b) the compromise to confidentiality, (c) the therapist as double agent, and (d) the concern for individual care versus care for the group of which the individual is a member.

THE MORAL INTENT OF HEALTH INSURANCE

Market forces exclude a substantial number of Americans from health care coverage (Brock, 1995); those who cannot pay or who are not receiving benefits from their employers or who are not covered by Medicare or Medicaid will not have health insurance. Many others will have very thin coverage.

The free market should not be dictating distribution of health care. Because the state of a person's health relates directly to his or her ability to function in society and take advantage of presented opportunities, health care cannot be seen as just another commodity. Proper and timely health care can prevent serious loss of function, pain and suffering, and premature loss of life. Our society places much emphasis on equality of opportunity, striving to offer each child basic educational programs and each citizen a just legal system. Basic medical care helps to provide equal opportunity. In addition, if we have a moral responsibility to prevent suffering by starvation or lack of shelter, we have an ethical obligation to help prevent loss of functioning resulting from lack of basic health care (Brock, 1995). The cost-containment, profit-driven, market-ruled systems do not provide a health safety net. It is up to government to create its own.

Given the acceptance of this premise, many difficult questions follow: What should the ideal benefit package contain? How much psychotherapy should be in it? What are society, government, and business willing to pay, and for whom? What is the value of each expenditure? How does one deal with different groups such as the chronically ill, the poor, and young, healthy individuals?

For example, should care of a chronically ill young man who is confined to a hospital bed, who cannot talk, and whose care cost exceeds the average annual wage of American workers be given higher priority than psychotherapeutic services for ten post-rape women? Although public policy questions rarely will be framed in this way, the more abstract policy decisions will pit the needs and desires of groups against each other as policymakers strive to find rational ways to contain costs.

Public policy continues to reevaluate the role of government in the health care of indigent people. If policymakers decide, for example, that paying for basic health care coverage becomes an individual choice, government and society must decide what to do about those who elect not to pay for their own health insurance and yet show up in the emergency room sick, injured, and uninsured. Without alternative plans, their costs would be paid by those who have purchased coverage. Individual responsibility for personal health would require clarification.

The revolution in health care is forcing individuals and providers to reevaluate their own abilities and decisions. The economic shifts in health care are moving individuals toward increased responsibility for personal health; specific policy decisions can further refine the specifics of individual responsibility for such problems as when to make an appointment with a specialist, psychotherapist, primary care physician, or primary care nurse.

More difficult ethical questions remain for health care policymakers as well as individual voters. For example, widely available and accepted euthanasia would certainly be cost-effective. The largest Medicare expenditures are for persons in the last few months of their lives, when intense and sometimes heroic medical procedures are initiated to prolong the lives of weakening bodies. Increasingly, people are also supporting the notion that "death on demand" can improve the quality of life by eliminating pain and suffering. On the other hand, MCOs rationally interested in cost containment may seek ways to encourage sick, frail, and pain-ridden clients to end their lives; the MCOs might do this to save money rather than as a humane gesture. Such inhumane thinking already has been illustrated in a few outstanding instances. For example, the case of a client with a severe leg infection was presented for treatment decision to an MCO. To treat the leg medically would have cost $90,000; to amputate would have cost $9,000. The MCO chose amputation to save money. The client, struggling for her limb, took the MCO to court and won her leg.

We may, in the very near future, see a similar dilemma in the treatment of major psychiatric disorders such as schizophrenia and bipolar disorders. Perhaps we will see the discovery of an expensive, highly effective medical or surgical treatment that could work for a small percentage of clients. We do not know, however, which patients would respond positively. The means to decide who receives the new treatment would have to be worked out carefully. Even now, some cost-conscious managers are forcing clinicians to use less expensive antipsychotics when the more expensive newer ones such as olanzapine, sertindole, and risperidone might be more helpful.

How are psychotherapeutic services to be rationed? The answer depends on the values of the payer. Should clients functioning at a 40% level receive services so that they might function at a 70% level, to the exclusion of clients functioning at 80% who could, with psychotherapy, function at 90%? Administrators of the federal government's entitlement programs might respond quite differently from representatives of large businesses. How much input to the decision is given to employees, to voters, and to Medicare beneficiaries? If these constituents are to be involved, policymakers must frame the objectives in economic or social values, asking what outputs from the program are desired. Are the objectives to be framed in economic terms, social terms, or others?

In many respects, letting free-market activities dictate who receives how much health care relieves social/governmental policymakers from very difficult decisions. On the other hand, capitalistic solutions to health care policy significantly disadvantage individuals already disadvantaged, widening the gap between the rich and the poor.

COMPROMISING CONFIDENTIALITY

Managed systems easily compromise confidentiality because case managers require information about specific clients. No longer can clients' files be private. For example, the 1996 case review form of Value Behavioral Health required therapists to include not only the client's name but also date of birth, social security number, address, home and work telephone numbers, and employer. All this information is already stored in the company's data bank. Why require it to be repeated on the same form as detailed descriptions of the client's problems and DSM-IV diagnosis? This confidentiality problem could be settled by assigning each client a number, so that case review could be confidential. Currently, for each authorized treatment, a personal identification number usually is assigned; nevertheless, many companies persist in using client names without any clear recognition or even explanation of why they insist on making it so easy to break confidentiality.

Some companies demand extensive reports and even copies of the records in order, they claim, to make informed decisions about how many sessions to authorize. Many clients unwittingly agree to this intrusion when they sign up for their HMO coverage. The fine print escapes their attention. (The general public also is ignorant of the fact that any judge at any time can subpoena supposedly confidential medical records.) Consequences can be disastrous. Although data concerning the negative effects of confidentiality breaches may never be available, clinical vignettes abound.

A man sought therapy out of guilt about his extramarital relationship. The MCO demanded complete copies of the therapist's records. Because the client had signed an agreement to release any and all records requested, the therapist felt obligated to release them. The MCO then sent a summary of the case with an authorization to the therapist, with a copy sent to the client's home. His wife opened the letter, read the purpose of his treatment, and sued for divorce.

Clients' rights to privacy are repeatedly being challenged.

Confidentiality problems within managed care will help to maintain a *private* practice market niche outside managed care. In it, records will be accessible to no one, except perhaps by court order.

THERAPISTS AS DOUBLE AGENTS

Like other health professionals, psychotherapists tend to resist the idea that psychotherapy practice is simply a business, producing and selling a product. The commercial language of daily discussions (covered lives, product line, market share, revenue streams, limited liability corporations) contradict the client-centered calling that drew most of us into the profession. Unlike most bankers, computer salespeople, or magazine publishers, for whom increasing profit margins remains the goal, psychotherapists have traditionally held the clients' increasing well-being as the primary target. The money followed. By doing good, one also did reasonably well (Brock, 1995).

The incentives to keep costs down can convince therapists to underutilize available resources or to undertreat clients in ways that could be harmful. For example, under several of the newer scenarios, depressed clients are more likely to be given antidepressants and followed up by their primary care physicians rather than being referred for psychotherapy. When is pharmacotherapy insufficient? When should psychotherapy be initiated first?

Some would argue that underutilization and undertreatment can be guarded against through the use of various quality monitoring and client outcome measurement systems that tie provider compensation to quality and outcome criteria. In addition, they would suggest that there is strong market pressure to provide high quality of care. If a system achieved cost savings at the expense of lower outcomes or lower satisfaction, then this system would be at a competitive disadvantage in the next round of contract negotiations. The crucial concept in the new economics of managed care could be value: the best outcome at the lowest price (after Shortell, 1994). The cost-containment motive nevertheless seems to be in the lead, with the value motive maintaining a distant second.

The demise of fee-for-service payment schemes with increasing reliance on capitation threatens two fundamental aspects of the psychotherapeutic relationship: trust and truth. Can anxious, vulnerable clients trust therapists, and can these therapists be truthful about treatments when the therapists are given incentives to recommend less treatment rather than more? Therapists in large and small systems increasingly will be encouraged to pay attention to profitability first and client care second. They will have legal responsibilities to shareholders to maximize profits or suffer the harsh disciplines of the marketplace (Brock, 1995). Continuing job security relies on responding to these market demands, especially if there is a glut of psychotherapists.

What if a client exceeds the benefit limits of the plan, yet still needs therapy because it is keeping him from killing himself? This major ethical and legal problem in managed care will need to be resolved by the courts. If the caseworker for the MCO refuses to grant more sessions, the therapist is obligated to appeal the decision to limit care. In general medicine, if a physician does not protest (Applebaum, 1993), then the full responsibility for any negligence in treatment, including lack of treatment, lies with the provider. If the managed care company refuses to pay for continued treatment and its termination results in client self-harm, and if the provider has protested, then the company could be responsible. Federal law protects some MCOs under the Employee Retirement Income Security Act (ERISA) from any major financial liability. The managed care company also can claim that limited treatment was all the employee/employer bought in the original agreement. If the therapist feels an obligation to the client and cannot find other care, then he or she may be forced to consider a fee reduction or face the uncertainty of legal action (should the client attempt or complete suicide). In any case, the therapist should be certain to register a formal protest with the managed care company.

Sometimes a clinically compassionate discussion with the case manager, who is permitted some flexibility, will yield the additional sessions, but only if these are permitted through the employer's benefit plan. The best argument from a therapist is centered on limiting or preventing the more costly inpatient stay.

Any kind of formal or informal protesting may spell trouble for providers. The following "gag" clause from an MCO contractual agreement provides a common illustration:

> Physician shall agree not to take any action or make any communication which undermines or could undermine the confidence of enrollees, potential enrollees, their employers, their unions or the public in US Healthcare (the MCO), or the quality of US Healthcare coverage, and physician shall keep the Proprietary Information (payment rates, utilization-review procedures, etc.), and this Agreement strictly confidential. (Woolhandler & Himmelstein, 1995)

Although some legislation has been enacted to eliminate such gag clauses, some MCOs have found ways to less directly muzzle provider complaints through threats to remove trouble-making providers from their panels.

Companies that include gag clauses undermine the therapeutic relationship by forcing practitioners to mislead some clients. A "gag" clause restricts providers' treatment options by preventing them from discussing noncovered services with a client. If, for example, the MCO permitted only the use of tricyclic antidepressants and did not permit the use of the more expensive, newer antidepressants, the provider might not be able to suggest these alternative drugs.

Therapists become *double agents* when they limit treatment sessions because they want to earn more for themselves while trying to operate in the client's best interest. Therapists will want to present a cost-effective profile. Clinicians' first ethical obligation is to serve their clients. Although financial gain is a motivator, clients' well-being comes first. Therapists may be pressured to forget their primary ethical obligation as managed care financial incentives and disincentives pull them from their role as client advocate.

A survey of 100 capitated physician groups found that physician-led managed care groups were adopting the same cost-cutting methods as business-run MCOs. Financial control was ranked by 62% of respondents as having the greatest influence on their group's utilization management strategy, whereas only 23% ranked quality of care as most important ("Physician-Led MCOs," 1996).

In 1995, in Simi Valley, California, two physicians were found guilty of placing their financial self-interest over the health of their clients. As part of an HMO contract, the physicians received $27 per month for every client who signed up with them. As part of the arrangement, they were obligated to pay for the specialty treatment for any client. A client died of colon cancer after having had her diagnostic workup delayed until it was too late for effective treatment. The jury ruled that financial concerns preempted the physicians from diagnosing an "obvious" colon cancer, which if treated early enough might not have cost the client her life. The debate about whether and how financial incentives can lead to malpractice will continue in the courts (Palermo, 1996).

We can assume that providers will revise their treatment decisions based on financial incentives. A therapist in private practice or group practice will be paid by a variety of mechanisms. Some clients will have regular insurance and pay the difference between what the insurance will cover and the fee. Some will pay the full fee. These groups may be treated differently. The ones who are paying the full fee themselves, with or without insurance copayment, may be kept in therapy longer, whereas those under managed care may have shortened therapy. Therapists need to judge what the MCO management is willing to tolerate. If a therapist lengthens treatment too often, the therapist may be dismissed from the panel. Reimbursement patterns for providers are strong shapers of provider behavior. Trying to negotiate the treacherous channel between client care and making a living raises serious ethical dilemmas for psychotherapists.

POPULATION VERSUS INDIVIDUAL CARE

A focus only on the individual client or family has passed. Formerly, physician and client (or therapist and client) decided in the relative isolation of the consulting room what their treatment arrangement would involve. Fair treatment of individuals is being replaced by fair treatment of populations: the greatest good for the greatest number.

The forms of managed care on the horizon require therapists to serve not two but three masters. In addition to serving the needs of cost containment and individual clients, therapists increasingly will be called to serve the population of which the client is a member. Population-oriented treatment will lead not only to prevention but also to questions about the proper expenditure of limited resources. Here provider, individual beneficiaries, and employer/payer confront the most difficult ethical issues. How many 93-year-olds should receive coronary artery bypass grafts? How many and which premature infants should receive intensive care? Which client should receive 40 sessions in place of 10 who could receive an average of 4 sessions each? Psychotherapy and medical/surgery care is now being rationed in a haphazard way. What is the most ethical way in which to distribute a limited resource? The answers will depend on the values defined and adopted by the various populations and their representatives.

These population-based ethical questions extend beyond mental and physical health benefits. How should resources to dependent populations who need housing, financial benefits, mental health treatment, and other support services be equitably distributed (Schlesinger, 1995)? Not only must direct treatment be considered in the formulation, but also how to finance and organize supported living and social casework (Surles, 1995).

Cost-containment efforts are eroding the primary psychotherapeutic emphasis on the individual. Population economics, financial incentives, and information needs of the bureaucracy all erode respect for individual autonomy and uniqueness. The psychotherapeutic emphasis on the individual has become a variable that requires political will to maintain.

CHAPTER 5

Effects of Cost Containment on Therapists, Practice, and Training

Cost containment efforts are shaping therapist role expectations, many practitioners are losing money ("MCOs Report Lower Fees," 1996) and control over their professional lives, therapists are being required to concentrate more closely on time and outcomes than ever before, the process of therapy is being reshaped by the entrance of third-party observers (case managers, financial monitors) into the therapeutic relationship, and professional schools training psychotherapists are perplexed about whom to train to do what.

PRACTITIONER REACTIONS TO MANAGED CARE

Once free to follow many different post-training professional paths, psychotherapists are witnessing a constriction of their options. Indemnity insurance fostered a proliferation of therapists, but cost containment is reversing that trend. No longer can new psychotherapists feel confident that they can establish solo private practices and have a sufficient number of clients to earn a satisfactory income. Reasons include lowered hourly fees, more hurdles to become eligible to serve on provider panels, and less money available for psychotherapy treatment.

Inherent in the term *manage* is the oversight function. Therapists have contentedly functioned in the privacy of their own offices, relatively immune to the probing eyes of the law and payers. Those doors are now being thrown open for managers to observe what once was private and confidential. When the private begins to become public, individuals become self-conscious. They begin to observe themselves, to notice what others also may be observing. This strange experience of being observed, which therapists experienced during training through process notes, videotapes, and one-way mirrors, now appears in professional life with strong financial implications.

The unnamed observers alter the conduct of therapy. Therapists are being required to hasten the therapy process, be more active, encourage more client responsibility, complete treatment plan forms that often require excessive detail, and accept resulting changes in the therapeutic relationship.

Therapist reactions have been very strong. Some describe managed care companies as predators:

> We are swimming with the greedy money-making sharks in an ocean of open marketplace competitiveness, and the sharks are tearing away. . . . (J. Cutler, quoted in Karel, 1995)

Others describe them as totalitarian:

> If the argument that the physician should take into account a role as "steward of society's resources" sounds familiar, it is because this was the central tenet of Nazi biomedical "ethics" (see Lifton's *The Nazi doctors* or Burleigh's *Death and Deliverance*). While it is a few steps from limiting the use of risperidone to simply killing the client for the sake of "stewarding society's resources," the steps are along an old familiar road. (Levitas, 1995)

Practitioners must spend their already scarce time requesting session frequency authorizations, arguing for psychotherapy when case managers insist on psychotropics, and distinguishing among differing benefit plans with their varying copayments and fee schedules. Practitioners may find different case managers operating under different rules in the same company. They must try to find flexible case managers versus those who just say "no." They must keep up with the continuing restructuring of the managed care businesses, as newly formed companies change the rules (again).

Despite these frustrations, a 1995 survey responded to by 250 readers of the *National Psychologist,* an independent newspaper for practitioners (Saeman, 1996b) revealed that almost 60% of practitioners continued to be in solo practice although many were disheartened and disgusted with the health care environment. Approximately 20% found their experience working with managed care "very unfavorable," 60% "unfavorable," 20% "favorable," and 1% "very favorable." This one exception was reported by a woman in solo practice who wrote, "My business is better than ever—wish (hope) it could stay the same; wouldn't change anything." Her earnings had tripled between 1990 and 1995. How or why was not mentioned. The average increase in income across respondents was 1.6% during the same period. As this finding might suggest, 82% were somewhat or very concerned about their professional futures, but only 20% had left their practices.

In 1994, psychiatrists' median income fell 1.4% to $108,000, placing them below pediatricians and family practitioners. Economic pressures have encouraged many to move to smaller towns. Some experienced New York City psychiatrists who had charged up to $150 per hour in previous years were, in 1995, accepting clients at $80 per hour (Hymowitz, 1995).

The psychotherapy professions are experiencing the grief that accompanies the loss of money and control. Humans grieve in part because they had expected that their relationship with the lost other would go on forever. Like no other event in the history of psychotherapy, the managed care revolution is forcing psychotherapists to acknowledge that we are more like our clients than we would like to think.

TIME-EFFECTIVE ATTITUDES

Therapists are being forced to learn new perspectives not usually taught by their professors. No longer is it sufficient to have gone through a training program and to be learning from experience to sharpen what already is understood. Therapists must innovate to stay even.

Therapy has to become shorter and more problem focused. Therapists are being asked for each presenting case to define a problem that can be solved. They generally will not be paid by MCOs to explore the client's past life and mind in subtle detail. Clients have increasingly greater responsibility for change. They may need to keep diaries, perhaps view videotapes of sessions, join support groups, involve family members and friends, and participate actively in sessions. The mysterious seems to be falling away from psychotherapy, at least under cost containment. "Efficient" and "effective"—these are the ideal watchwords, although the underlying theme often is simply to do more with less. Therapists are learning new definitions of words that they must use in their practices, like "focal therapy," "impairments," "progress notes," and "treatment plan." Therapists also are learning new self-talk.

NEW SELF-INSTRUCTIONS
FOR THERAPISTS

Following are some specific emerging forms of self-talk.

a. Do just enough therapy to facilitate the beginning of change. Help people get started in the right direction, then bow out by lengthening intervals between sessions or stopping. Those therapists wedded to weekly to long-term therapy instead of monthly or biweekly, or those needing a sense of certainty about change before suggesting termination, find this instruction problematic.

b. Seize the rapid change opportunity of the first session or two. The early sessions provide the greatest opportunity for change. Although more therapy is usually associated with more change, the greatest increments of change per session come during the first few sessions (Howard, Kopta, Krause, & Orlinsky, 1986).

c. Know your limits. Just because you cannot help does not mean someone else cannot. Acknowledge the limits of your psychotherapy skills. Don't be afraid to rapidly refer or consult.

d. Don't ignore the obvious. If a client has multiple bruises, ask about them. If the client suddenly begins to cry, ask about it. If the client has a major impairment, objectively pursue understanding it.

e. Grasp a limited focus and stay with it. Avoid too much rambling and wandering. Define patterns to change and stay with them. Passive, reflective listening deserves less than 25% of a brief therapy hour (Sloane, Cristol, Pepernik, & Whipple, 1975).

f. Explore what leads to positive changes as well as what leads to negative ones. Instead of delving only into the details surrounding negative occurrences, be just as curious about what led to no fighting, no binge eating, no drinking, or no depressive reaction. Build on the positive behaviors, attitudes, and experiences contributing to the more desirable outcomes.

g. Avoid engaging in causal arguments with clients. You are arguing only from theoretical bias and are wasting time. Find descriptions of events that you both can understand that lead to suggestions about what to change. Attempt to confirm clients' explanations unless your alternative implies a more efficient solution (M. A. Hubble, personal communication, January 26, 1994).

h. Invent homework assignments. The assignment of homework offers a clear message to clients: Use the other 167 hours in the week for your own work on yourself. Therapeutic relationships that emphasize change only through the relationship with the therapist and that exclude work outside the office are likely to take longer and to miss emphasizing change experiences outside the office work.

INFLUENCE OF COST CONTAINMENT
ON THE PROCESS OF PSYCHOTHERAPY

The apparently wide distinctions among the schools of psychotherapy have impelled some therapists to search for the basic concepts that hold the schools together. Most therapists seem to agree that psychotherapy is a process and that this process moves through predictable stages. Therapist and client(s) develop a working alliance (engagement/assessment), define dysfunctional patterns (pattern search), often experience transference and countertransference, initiate change, and then terminate (Beitman, 1987). The conduct of each of these stages is being altered by cost containment measures.

Engagement/Assessment

To some clients, the therapist's inclusion or exclusion from a provider panel may be improperly equated to the therapist's competence (Saakvitne & Abrahamson, 1994) and may therefore call into question the therapist's competence should the therapist not be on a certain panel. The managed care paradigm requires therapists to establish trust quickly and to define a diagnosis quickly. Most plans require that the identified client have a DSM-IV Axis I diagnosis as well as an indication of severity usually Axis V (American Psychiatric Association, 1996) and a treatment plan. Therapists usually are asked to predict how many sessions treatment will take and the outcome measures that will indicate successful treatment.

The therapeutic contract defines the relationship between therapist and client as well as the relationship between the dyad and those outside. The rules of managed care include a third-party viewer (who in more mature systems will be the organization of which the therapist is a member). The case manager assumes the authority to determine how many sessions will take place, a decision previously made within the psychotherapy dyad. For clients who are deeply sensitive to interpersonal loss and abandonment, the uncertainty of future contacts because of MCO decisions can inhibit the development of trust. After all, case managers are empowered to terminate or shorten treatment within the benefits structure.

The loss of autonomy associated with the new intrusion on therapists creates frustration and helplessness. Therapists may feel devalued and humiliated by the review process and angry that the person directing therapy probably has less training and experience than they do. Clients may experience the review process as one more difficult hurdle to overcome and as reinforcement of the stigma associated with seeking mental health treatment. Both may feel ignored in a system that places profit and cost savings ahead of the mutuality found in the therapeutic dyad (Saakvitne & Abrahamson, 1994).

For psychoanalytically oriented psychotherapy, these strictures are particularly painful because of its emphasis on meaning as it unfolds in the transference. Classic psychoanalytic approaches require that managed care third parties (like any third party) be excluded from participation so as not to distort the transference and countertransference. For those therapists who include managed care payers and carefully track these psychodynamic issues, transference as well as countertransference responses to managed care intrusions may add useful material for interpretation as described in the section below discussing pattern search.

Pattern Search

In most therapeutic relationships, therapists define patterns of thought, feeling, and/or action of the client(s) that, if changed, would lead to a desirable outcome. Under cost-containment systems, therapists have relatively less exploratory time to define a problem focus than they had in the past.

Complex clients are not easily put into psychotherapeutic diagnostic categories. For those cases, instead of diagnosis, therapists will be required to quickly define patterns that could be worked on, hoping that correction in one pattern can cascade into changes in others. Unfortunately, these hopes are unlikely to be realized in a substantial subgroup of complex clients (Gabbard, 1997).

Another alternative to long-term weekly therapy for difficult clients is to spread the few sessions allotted to these clients over many months. Primary care physicians, family members, and self-help groups can contribute their resources as well. When sessions are spaced apart, therapists need to take good notes to remember what has been discussed from one session to the next.

For borderline clients, this brief intermittent contact may prove to be costly rather than cost-effective. One study (Hoke, 1989) described 58 borderline clients who were followed for up to 7 years. Two different groups were evident: Approximately half had intermittent or inconsistent therapy contacts, and the other half had consistent psychotherapy over at least 2 years. The second group showed greater improvement in mood functioning, a decreased need for more intensive treatment (such as emergency room visits, hospitalization, and day treatment), decreased impulsiveness, and improved global functioning. It may be more cost-effective for systems to provide extended, consistent treatment for these clients (Gabbard, 1997).

Transference and Countertransference

Like any shift in the therapeutic relationship, cost containment can trigger transference reactions including the following.

1. *Bad case manager and good therapist.* The therapist may join the client in accusing a case manager of malicious intent. Anger that might be directed toward the therapist is directed at the manager, and the therapist becomes idealized. If the psychoanalytic goal of therapy is to help clients integrate both the devalued and idealized parts of others and the self through transference analysis, then this splitting may create a therapeutic stalemate. The client blames the case manager who remains All Bad. The client forgives the therapist who remains All Good. The client then never has the opportunity to assimilate the fact that the therapist has both All Good and All Bad qualities, just like the client himself.

2. *Therapist as nonprotective witness.* For clients who have been abused, the therapist may appear as a bystander to the intrusive control of managed care. If benefits can be revoked or reduced, then the therapist observes without apparently intervening on the client's behalf.

3. *Therapist as victim.* The therapist may be seen as a victim of powerful forces, thus evoking sympathy, identification, contempt, despair, and possibly guilt in the client. Over time, the client can experience the therapist as helpless and weak.

In reality, the therapist is neither victim nor passive observer of the system, but to the extent the therapist shares the client's beliefs, the relationship can be stalemated. If, however, the client persists in believing that the therapist is also a victim of this new system, then the reality of the therapist's autonomy becomes lost and, with it, the client's potential autonomy.

Therapists may attempt unconsciously to rid themselves of their uncomfortable feelings of helplessness and/or frustration by projecting them onto their clients, who would then appear more victimized.

Therapists may be relieved when clients express anger at case managers rather than themselves (Saakvitne & Abrahamson, 1994).

Change

Because of the need for rapid results, therapists need to marshal several different change processes. Therapists who demonstrate speedy effectiveness will be allowed to continue as members of managed care networks. Overseers monitor the therapist's personal statistics, particularly costs incurred through session frequency per client and client satisfaction.

Therapists may find themselves pushing their clients to change well before they are ready, simply to please the managed care company statisticians. For those who believe in long-term unfolding, direct focus on symptom reduction may mean too rapid closure of the therapeutic relationship. Calm and permissive listening that encourages transference development may be viewed by cost-efficiency managers as ineffective treatment (Saakvitne & Abrahamson, 1994).

Termination

Under managed care, the end is in sight during the initial evaluation. Not too long ago, trainees were encouraged to develop "long-term cases" to mimic Freud's psychoanalytic procedure as developed by his followers. There is much to be gained by long-term psychotherapeutic relationships involving the many subtle complexities of transference and countertransference. Under managed care, however, therapists work under time limits. They might ask for additional sessions, but often they will not get them. They can appeal, or they can ask the client to pay, perhaps by dramatically reducing the fee. Otherwise, there will be little time for the useful niceties of termination.

On the other hand, pressure of a quick termination persuades some clients to engage more actively in the change process, forcing them to utilize therapeutic time in more effective ways. No longer do clients interested in "just talking" have as easy access to a friendly, compassionate ear.

Limited session work may work in a therapist's favor: He or she may use managed care as an excuse to terminate unwanted clients. The therapist may not try particularly hard to secure more sessions, and an outside hand will appear to have shortened the relationship.

EFFECTS OF COST CONTAINMENT
ON TRAINING

The fate of psychotherapy education is likely to parallel the fate of medical school education because therapists, like physicians, seem to be in oversupply. In addition, health care educators, like psychotherapy educators, have tended to resist absorbing and adapting to the cost-containment environment, making them more vulnerable to cost-cutting efforts. From some quarters, there is little sympathy for American Medical Centers (and by implication other health workforce institutions; Fox, 1995).

The following Pew Commission (1995) recommendations concerning the projected number of medical students and residents might help to awaken leaders of psychotherapy training programs.

1. Reduce the number of graduate medical training positions (residents) to the number of U.S. medical school graduates plus 10% because about 35% of all residents in training in the United States are graduates of non-U.S. medical schools.
2. By 2005, reduce the size of the entering medical school class in the United States by 20-25%. This would mean a reduction from the 1995 class of 17,500 to an entering class size of 13,000 to 14,000 for 2005. The reductions in graduate training positions described in item 1 should move downward with the reduction in medical school class size. *This reduction should come from closing down medical schools, not reducing class size.* (emphasis added)

Perhaps recommendations like these will be extended to the training of psychotherapists. Some programs will close because potential therapists, reacting to apparent market pressures, will select other careers. Some programs will be closed by university administrations or state legislatures that recognize that enough therapists have been trained.

Pressure by the federal government has strongly influenced psychotherapy training in medical schools. In 1996, the Health Care Financing Administration (HCFA) ruled that beginning July 1, 1996, psychiatric residents could no longer charge Medicare to do psychotherapy without the presence and involvement of a teaching physician, who must be present or view the resident's service (through a one-way mirror or on video camera) for the time period required by the billing code. Psychiatric training programs are no longer able to bill for psychotherapy on the resident's initiative alone. Instead, the attending physician is required to work side by side with each resident instead of seeing his or her own clients at the same time and supervising later. This ruling followed closely after HCFA reduced the amount of money medical schools received for their residency training programs. The effect is that psychiatric residents will do less and less psychotherapy, especially in those programs that must generate money for their services.

With reductions in health care expenditures to hospitals and medical schools, psychology internship programs could be threatened. With a reduction in postdoctoral placements, many PhD candidates will have difficulty finishing their required training. Some will earn PhDs but be prevented from practicing because of limitations on the number of internships.

The mental health professions may have spawned vocational trauma. Many people have been attracted to perform psychotherapy so that individual session costs escalated. Competition among therapists did not bring costs down among individual practitioners under standard fee-for-service. Instead, costs for individual sessions went up, in part because new therapists had higher debt loads and needed to make more money than experienced therapists to pay off their debts. The market absorbed those increases. New therapists will now be part of systems that will determine salaries and per-session fees. There will be less money for psychotherapy than there would have been without cost controls. Cost per session will not go up as it has in the past few decades. Position numbers in cost-containing systems will be limited.

Graduate training programs in psychotherapy must begin to consider the painful process of trimming the apparent excess of practitioners. Unfortunately, faculty of training institutes tend to feel immune from the power of managed care, leaving their students to search for guidance from teachers who feel untouched by these strong shifting winds of change. Perhaps only follow-up data from unemployed graduates will change their course structures. Without policy decisions, the marketplace will dictate the downsizing of practitioner cohorts and training programs.

The heated debates and anxiety generated by cost containment will bring about change in the content of training programs. Because managed care requires increasing attention to outcome data, training programs will be required to teach how to collect and report such data. Training program directors, like psychotherapists in practice, will feel the pressure to organize efficient and effective experiences that demonstrate that students are learning what they are expected to know. Yet more difficult, but also necessary, is demonstrating that what they learn, they practice, and what they practice is both efficient and effective. If training programs do not attend to outcome measurements, then psychotherapy will be further battered by the many different influences working to break it apart. (See Chapter 6 for a discussion of these influences.)

Training programs also ignore the very real fact that some people should not become psychotherapists. Proper screening could identify those with the greatest potential. Evidence from one family therapy training program suggested that 50% of the outcome variance was related to factors outside the training program and inherent in the experiences of the trainees. For example, it appeared that trainees with spouses and children scored significantly better than those without a family (Breunlin et al., 1989). Clearly, some individuals are more effective at establishing and maintaining relationships than others. How much can a training program expect to increase relationship building skills? What else does it take to become a good therapist? The answers include strong motivation, compassion for others, desire to listen well, a degree of practical knowledge about how to live in the world, and an ability to continue to adapt to changes in society, clients, and oneself (Guy, 1987). Criteria for the basic essentials of effective therapists could be developed for use in determining entrance qualifications.

Simply having a reputation as a good training program in psychotherapy will no longer be sufficient for survival. To determine the number of training sites and the number of trainees to be graduated from them, data may need to be collected to suggest the optimal number of therapists for a given locality. National accrediting organizations will ensure that training programs are providing sufficient information about managed care to provide their graduates a running start in the cost-containment environment. Trainees will need to understand business, government, information systems, population treatment, and cost-containment ethics—as well as psychotherapy—in this new era.

WHAT PSYCHOTHERAPISTS CAN DO FOR THEMSELVES AND THEIR CLIENTS

We can manage change by developing coherent views of the desired future. To know what to do in the future, we begin by delineating the current strengths and weaknesses of psychotherapy. A major strength of psychotherapy lies in the strong support research has given to its efficacy. Chief among the weaknesses is the lack of understanding by practicing psychotherapists of this strong research support for the value of psychotherapy. Knowledge of this information can help to convert passive, frightened practitioners into armed citizen-professional-politicians. Bolstered by this confidence-inspiring data, therapists can more readily confront threats from the outside (like pharmacotherapy-only approaches and antipsychotherapy legislation) as well as threats from the inside (such as excess numbers of therapists, professional and theory-based dissent, ineffective therapists, and process research versus manual-based research acrimony). Imaginative efforts to diminish these influences will pave the way toward a clear plan defining the place of psychotherapy within the health care system as described in Chapter 6.

To foster the development of more effective psychotherapeutic practices, therapists will venture outside their offices to link increasingly more closely with general medicine and with self-help groups. In addition, a variety of important political actions will need to be considered, as described in Chapter 7. After venturing out into their communities, psychotherapists can then return to their offices to think anew about what they do there. They must be much more clever at business, understand contracts, participate in network development, and adapt to the ever-changing environment by being ready to keep changing (Chapter 8). This section and the book end with a peek into the practice of psychotherapy in the 21st century, when outcomes measurement will take center stage.

6

Confronting Key Problems for Psychotherapy

Psychotherapists generally lack confidence in their effectiveness. As individuals, they are able to look to dramatic and useful results from their caseloads, but generally they are ignorant of the tremendous body of knowledge supporting psychotherapy efficacy. Psychotherapy works! Know the literature and advertise it! Use this data in efforts to counter threats from both inside and outside psychotherapy. Strive to minimize these threats. Then try to answer this most difficult question: Which people with what kinds of problems in which settings should receive what psychotherapeutic help from which therapists?

THE EFFICACY AND COST-EFFECTIVENESS OF PSYCHOTHERAPY

The prevailing opinion holds that psychopharmacological interventions have demonstrated efficacy and that psychotherapeutic interventions have not. In fact, there is a considerable amount of data to suggest that psychotherapy in many forms demonstrates *efficacy*, meaning that under controlled research conditions, it usually outperforms a control group on measures of symptom change. Psychotherapists can take heart from these data, which are summarized here. Both pharmacotherapy and psychotherapy interventions, however, have only recently been forced to be tested for *effectiveness*, which refers to how well they perform in the real clinical world, with measurement usually concerning quality of life, work, and social adjustment. A crucial subcategory of effectiveness is *cost-benefit*, which depends heavily on how "benefit" is defined (e.g., symptoms, work functioning, social functioning, recurring medical or psychiatric costs, relapse, family satisfaction, or reduction in cost to society).

Psychotherapy can be a significant contributor to healthy lives, especially lives under stress. Diet, exercise, and meditation each receive remarkable media attention. A few famous individuals praise the lifesaving effects of long-term psychotherapy. Rarely, however, do psychotherapists proclaim the well-established fact that brief therapy helps many people very much. Four to eight sessions can turn around the lives of some people. The cost? Less than the yearly membership in many health clubs. Psychotherapy should be considered along with diet and exercise as a means to physical and psychological well-being in a healthy society.

Meta-analytic outcomes studies have demonstrated strong positive effects of psychotherapy in a variety of conditions including anxiety disorders and depression, comparing favorably to coronary artery bypass surgery and demonstrating greater effects than drug treatments for arthritis and anticoagulant therapies (Lipsey & Wilson, 1993). A large body of research has demonstrated efficacy of various manualized forms of psychotherapy based on school-specific treatment approaches. The treatment studies compare favorably in design and results to pharmacotherapy (see Frank, Karp, & Rush, 1993 for review of studies of both pharmacotherapy and psychotherapy for depression). There is much more evidence for psychotherapy's efficacy.[1]

There is also much data suggesting that psychotherapy has a beneficial impact on costs. Many studies demonstrate decreased medical utilization following mental health intervention (e.g., fewer doctor's office visits, fewer hospitalizations, fewer lab and x-ray procedures). Few studies have examined the actual cost offsets, if any, associated with mental health interventions. How much less is the cost of mental health intervention compared to the *cost savings* of the intervention?

Unfortunately, medical cost offset studies are relatively old. In addition, the cost savings were primarily related to reductions in inpatient days; these findings are less relevant because cost containment already has forced significant reductions.[2]

To consider the *cost-effectiveness* generated by psychotherapy requires that a desirable chain of events be initiated: improved self-management, reduced symptoms, and more effective social interactions, all leading to reduced treatment costs and better economic functioning. These are, indeed, stringent requirements! Some recent evidence suggests, nevertheless, that data for such effects do exist, especially in the psychotherapeutic treatment of schizophrenia, bipolar disorder, and borderline personality. Much of the economic impact comes from reductions in psychiatric inpatient treatment and decreases in work impairment (Gabbard, Lazar, Hornberger, & Spiegel, 1997).

Armed with data supporting the efficacy and effectiveness of psychotherapy and the various forms of cost-benefit analysis that shape the debate about the value of this service, therapists can enter the political arena to advocate for psychotherapy and its clients.

THREATS FROM OUTSIDE PSYCHOTHERAPY

Many of the challenges to psychotherapy lie outside its practice and are beyond the threats of cost containment. Stigma against mental illness and its treatment continues, proposed anti-psychotherapy laws appears regularly in state and federal legislatures, and the pharmaceutical industry quietly continues to disparage psychotherapy in favor of drug treatment. Each may be confronted and diminished through group and individual action.

Stigma

Mental health benefit coverage has suffered perpetual discrimination under fee-for-service as well as managed care. Traditional insurance plans and HMOs have usually restricted mental health benefits more tightly than their medical care benefits by setting tighter limits on inpatient days and outpatient visits as well as by imposing lifetime and annual dollar limits (Boyle & Callahan, 1995).

This discrimination arises from several sources. The general public has preferred to believe that mental illness is a matter of choice (after all, it is *mental* illness). Because it is a choice, people are responsible for their own problems and should not be helped by society. Furthermore, the public has yet to distinguish clearly between the major mental illnesses (such as schizophrenia and bipolar disorder) and the lesser disorders (such as major depression and obsessive-compulsive disorder). This lumping together creates in the public mind a view that all mentally ill are severely disturbed. In addition, some supporters within the mental health profession try to fight for benefits that include only the major mental illnesses. Compounding these swirling confusions is the continuing public perception that most clients entering psychotherapy stay in therapy for many years, a belief clearly contradicted by the fact that the average number of sessions for the past 30 years is between four and eight (Garfield, 1994). In addition, crimes committed by the mentally ill and fraud perpetrated by mental health service deliverers seem to attract excessive attention, turning the public's attitude yet more negative. Finally, the arguments among various theoretical orientations only confuse the public further (Boyle & Callahan, 1995). Despite evidence that the public is coming to accept the interrelationship between mind, brain, and body (e.g., Weil, 1995), the momentum built up over years of discrimination helps to prevent any major alterations in mental health coverage. Too many prognosticators have added to the problem by projecting unrealistically large cost overruns by mental health benefit parity despite evidence to the contrary (Schlesinger, 1995).

The public is coming to accept that the brain is the organ of the mind and that the brain strongly influences the health of the body. Individuals are recognizing that a healthy mind leads to a healthy brain, and a healthy brain leads to a healthy body. Furthermore, a healthy mind leads to healthy interactions, supportive social networks, and increased well-being and effectiveness (Pope, 1997). The old, heavy inertia of past discrimination against mental illness can be more easily overcome now than at any time in the past.

Anti-Psychotherapy Legislative Initiatives

Legislators in several states regularly see proposed laws, driven by energetic supporters of the "false memory syndrome," that could severely regulate the practice of psychotherapy. Hailed as "consumer protection," these laws require that before any therapeutic relationship begins, the therapist must present each client with a series of research articles describing the "procedure" to be undertaken and the "scientific" proof that this procedure is effective. These "experimentally validated therapies" (EVTs) (see the next section of this chapter) would then become the only ones available for therapists to use. Failure to inform clients properly would lead to lawsuits, revocation of license to practice, and public condemnation. Such legislation would strangulate psychotherapy practice.

The general public likes to think that medical interventions are science based and that services are absolutely reliable. To some extent they are, but the 1978 report of the federal Office of Technology Assessment found that only 10-20% of all medical procedures have been shown by controlled tests to be beneficial (quoted in Dorken & Pallak, 1994). The percentage has not changed much since then. Much treatment is based on fad and fashion because data to prove the effectiveness of many medical interventions is based on small studies often contradicting previous other small studies.

The false memory syndrome (FMS) debate and other attacks on psychotherapy require that the truth in the exaggerated claims by FMS advocates be acknowledged: namely, that there are many therapists whose work is faulty in that they encourage the construction of false memories of sexual abuse in the absence of such events. On the other hand, some people do repress memories of childhood abuse only to have them re-emerge in therapy (Zola, 1997). Legislation that strangulates psychotherapeutic practice will not provide an equitable solution to these problems.

The Pharmaceutical Industry

In more quiet ways, drug companies strive to divert the attention of consumers and payers from the beneficial effects of psychotherapy. In the treatment of depression, medications appear necessary for the more severe end of the spectrum, but they are of equal benefit in the aggregate for moderate depression. Placebos do as well as either pharmacotherapy or psychotherapy for mild depression (Elkin, 1996).

Drug companies attempt to persuade consumers that the diagnoses for which medications have obtained Federal Drug Administration (FDA) approval (e.g., depression, manic-depression, schizophrenia, panic disorder, obsessive-compulsive disorder, and generalized anxiety disorder) are *brain* diseases and therefore should be treated with chemicals. Most consumers and payers readily believe that a brain disease should be treated with a chemical while a mind disease should be treated mentally, that is, with psychotherapy. Increasingly more evidence from neuroimaging is demonstrating that thoughts have a basis in the brain and that new forms of thinking can permanently change brain function (Schwartz, 1996; Schwartz, Stoessel, Baxter, Martin, & Phelps, 1996). This perspective is subversive to drug company plans because it permits words to cross from the mind into the brain.

Drugs also appear to be less expensive than psychotherapy. This claim is difficult to refute. Psychotherapy sessions generally cost more than pharmacotherapy sessions plus medications. Psychotherapy researchers are then required to prove that psychotherapy clients do not relapse as often as those who take medications and discontinue them. That fewer clients relapse after discontinuing psychotherapy has been clearly demonstrated in the treatment of obsessive-compulsive disorder (Pato, Zohar-Kadouch, Zohar, & Murphy, 1988). The relative cost of long-term medication use compared with the cost of short-term psychotherapy may then be reversed. Unfortunately, such studies are enormously expensive to conduct and drug companies have little incentive to do them. Because the data to support the long-term cost-effectiveness of psychotherapy are unlikely to be developed, the side with the greatest advertising clout is the probable winner.

Many drug companies appear to recognize that combining treatments is likely to be beneficial in a subset of clients. Many representatives personally recognize that mind and words have valuable therapeutic effects; from a public perception perspective, many companies recognize the value that mental health treatment consumers place on psychotherapy. It is possible to promote the benefits of psychotherapy with drug company partners. Drug company symposia, for example, at various national and regional meetings of psychiatrists and psychologists—involving different diagnostic categories from depression to schizophrenia—often include psychotherapy research and clinical findings because the audience wants a balanced view.

Table 6.1 Mental Health Professionals in the State of Missouri

Type of Professional	Number	Number per 100,000 Population
Psychiatrists	1,721	32.5
Psychologists	1,696	32.1
Licensed clinical social workers	4,175	79
Certified psychiatric nurse specialists	70	1.3
Licensed professional counselors	1,483	28.1

THREATS FROM INSIDE

Perhaps the greater danger to psychotherapy practice lies within psychotherapy politics.

Too Many Therapists?

The American Psychiatric Association recommends approximately one psychiatrist per 10,000 people, and the American Psychological Association recommends approximately one psychologist per 10,000 population. There are no readily available data suggesting numbers for master's level therapists. The state of Missouri, as an example, has a population of about 5,300,000, so approximately 530 psychiatrists and 530 psychologists would be necessary. The actual numbers of mental health providers in 1995 are provided in Table 6.1.

These figures suggest that Missouri has about 170 mental health professionals for every 100,000 people. Not all of these people practice full-time, nor are all of them working as direct mental health providers. Many are administrators or researchers, or work in non-mental-health settings. Not included in these numbers are unlicensed practitioners.

Given the guild estimates from the American Psychiatric Association and American Psychological Association, Missouri has about three times as many psychiatrists and psychologists as it needs. Other estimates suggest that Missouri may need only three psychiatrists per 100,000, thus leading to a 10-fold excess. Because distribution is not even, rural areas still may lack coverage (D. Wedding, personal communication, January 31, 1996).

Projections of psychiatric (and other mental health workforce) needs depend on the design and structure of the health care systems in which workers function. Using the staff model HMO, for example, the need for psychiatrists would fall from the 35,000 practicing in 1994 to 10,000, or a surplus of about 25,000 (Wiener, 1994). Key variables for determining the number of psychotherapists include the model of access to care (gatekeeper vs. self-referral); the distribution of responsibilities among primary care physicians, psychiatrists, and other mental health disciplines; and the method for determining mental health benefits as well as the mental health portion of general health care expenditures. Projections also must include consideration of state, public, and forensic systems, as well as the federal Department of Veterans Affairs, because these systems service groups with higher rates of use, disability, and need for psychiatric, social, and medical services than the general population (Meyer & Sotsky, 1995).

The approximately 180 psychiatric training programs pour out more than 1,000 new psychiatrists a year; we now have six times as many psychiatrists in the United States as we had in 1965 (Fink, 1995). Should psychiatrists do the work residents are doing instead of training new ones? Should faculty members of social work and psychology departments extend their practices and reduce their teaching loads? The answer to these questions appears to be "yes."

These figures suggest that there should be fewer mental health professionals and fewer working therapists. Perhaps 10-30% of therapists currently in practice will find other employment, and another 10-20% will mix their practices with other forms of work as suggested in Chapter 8. Salaries and fees-for-service generally will be reduced, although cleverness and risk taking will greatly reward some. In a related development, supply and demand pressures for specialists in cardiology, pulmonology, and gastroenterology have been driving down earnings of these medical specialists. The likely effect on psychotherapy is that earnings will remain static as therapists work longer hours to maintain the same income (Saeman, 1996b). If therapist supply does not reduce, then therapists are more likely to fight each other for economic survival, resulting in a diminution of reputation and effectiveness of us all.

The Experimentally Validated
Therapies (EVTs) Controversy

Legislation that threatens to severely restrict psychotherapeutic practice moves forward in part because some psychotherapy researchers support limiting psychotherapy practice to only empirically validated therapies (Clement, 1996) despite the fact that most therapists are eclectic or integrative (Lambert & Bergin, 1994; Norcross & Goldfried, 1992). Psychotherapy will continue to become more research based, but significant evidence from meta-analytic studies of existing research suggests that psychotherapy in the aggregate, across schools and forms, is effective (Lipsey & Wilson, 1993). Supporters of EVT legislation neglect the limitations of their conclusions.[3] They neglect the research that supports the powerful impact of common factors, and they generalize too easily from research diagnosis to diagnostic problems in clinical practice. By suggesting that these EVTs are the only effective treatments, they stifle innovation.

The conflicts between clinicians and researchers and between process researchers and technique-focused researchers can be settled by recognizing that clinicians and researchers each have part of the solution and that school-specific techniques and common factors each contribute to the outcome variance (Lambert & Bergin, 1994).

Impaired and Unethical Practitioners

The normal curve for the continuum of "good-bad" therapists suggests that a small but important percentage of practitioners performs poorly. The American Medical Association reports that 3-10% of U.S. physicians perform poorly. Some effort has been made to discipline incompetent, impaired, or criminal physicians. In 1995, 3,800 physicians were disciplined, approximately 0.5% of the total number. About 950 of these actions led to suspension or revocation of licensure. Insurance fraud and other criminal actions were the most commonly reported abuses, followed closely by substandard care, misprescribing or overprescribing medications, and substance abuse. About 12% were sanctioned for sexual involvement with their clients (Stearley, 1996).

Much less is being done to limit the practices of incompetent or criminal psychotherapists. In addition to the damage caused by sexual involvement with clients, therapists exploit and mismanage in many different ways. Some cannot empathize well. Some are impatient, too authoritative, or directive. Some are poorly adjusted to their own lives, tend to see clients as people to serve their own needs, lack a sense of proper timing for interventions, and/or are frightened by severe pathology. About 10% of therapists themselves report having been harmed by their own participation as clients in psychotherapy (Grunebaum, 1985; reported in Lambert & Bergin, 1994).

The media exploit the reality of bad therapy by building stories around it. All therapists are painted by the same negative brush, and the quiet successes of the majority are lost to public view.

Psychotherapy professions have provided little energy to enforce their ethical guidelines. There are no major national laws governing the practice of psychotherapy. Most states have organized boards with varying power and jurisdictions. Mechanisms must be developed to identify and reject from practice people who are harmful to their clients. The numbers do not appear to be great, but the stigma associated with mental health treatment amplifies the bad news. The state of Colorado has a useful model to oversee and manage bad practitioners that other states might consider.[4]

In 1986, the National Practitioner Data Bank was established to track incompetent and illegal physicians as a means of helping to remove them from practice. This computer data bank details reports of physician malpractice, substandard care, license revocation, and other disciplinary actions. This unfortunately necessary bow to computer surveillance may help the careful pruning of psychotherapist ranks.

Professional Conflicts

The unfortunate wars among psychotherapy professions, particularly between psychiatry and clinical psychology, only damage mental health treatment. Focusing on petty struggles for power and money distracts from taking care of client needs. The continuing tragedy of such struggles lies in the fact that those fighting for territory tend not to be clinicians but rather politicians who appear more concerned with extension of power or threats to dominion than with client care.

The psychotherapy professions face the same challenges being confronted by cardiac surgeons who compete with cardiologists, ophthalmologists who compete with optometrists, and primary care nurses who compete with primary care physicians: how to cooperate for optimal care of clients while maintaining personal and professional strength. To accomplish psychotherapy enhancing initiatives, the various mental health professions must find ways to minimize their destructive infighting. One psychiatric leader in our community has been labeled "psychotic with a paranoid core" by his psychology competitors because he is a leader among the psychiatrists. The rage must be directed elsewhere. Grassroots efforts to bring the mental health professions together raise hopes that this destructive squabbling can be replaced by genuine efforts at reconciliation accompanied by strong advocacy for the mentally ill. While psychologists fight for prescription privileges and psychiatrists counter them, managed care has brought some psychiatrists and psychologists together. Certainly, if the two have a common "enemy," then the enemy of my enemy becomes my friend (Saeman, 1996a).

When therapists organize, they become a political constituency. Therapists also can join with other providers (nonpsychiatric physicians' hospitals, outpatient clinics, long-term care facilities) to increase their political leverage. When therapists organize with their clients and families, they become a larger political constituency. Some coalitions have formed to create an "Any Willing Provider" law. The intent of this law is to prohibit managed care plans from excluding qualified providers who are willing to meet the plan's terms, fees, utilization rules, and quality standards. The provision of choice for clients provides a rallying point for legislative action. Organizers of these political efforts must plan well ahead, develop testimony that health care costs will not increase astronomically because more providers are being managed, and include strong representation by client advocacy groups. MCOs, however, can find ways around "Any Willing Provider" laws by, for example, contracting with Exclusive Provider Organizations that then pick panel members.

Managed care companies can be monitored themselves. As various agencies seek to produce mental health report cards to determine what shall be measured as part of efficient and effective operations, professional groups can develop report cards for managed care companies. The Managed Care Report Card project seeks to profile managed care companies using key indicators such as amount and type of paperwork, character of the case managers, use and type of practice guide-lines, psychotherapy session limits, and medication type limits (Kaplan, 1996). In addition, many managed care companies do not have accurate data on utilization and costs. They simply take in money and limit access. Employers and providers may wish to know which companies do and do not have this information.

No Working Definition of Psychotherapy

Psychotherapy is not a profession. A profession is defined by a basic standard of principles and behavior endorsed by the professional organization itself. There is no single psychotherapy profession, and there are no professional standards for the practice of psychotherapy. At best, there are state laws regulating what cannot be done rather than what is to be done.

No clear, commonly accepted working definition has been adopted. We talk about psychotherapy, yet there is no clear agreement about what psychotherapy is.

If therapists are to defend psychotherapy against attacks and probing questions, therapists need to be able to share a common language, to be clear that they are saying the same things to the general public and politicians as well as to managed care companies. Therapists need to demonstrate that we know what we are doing. Psychotherapy can be defined in simple but comprehensive terms for these varying interest groups (see Beitman, 1997, for an example).

THE PLACE OF PSYCHOTHERAPY IN THE AMERICAN HEALTH CARE SYSTEM

Psychotherapists can influence policy decisions when armed with a purpose. Psychotherapists should define values that can be fashioned into laws that benefit psychotherapy clients.

What Is Health Insurance?

A basic question is "What is the purpose of health insurance?" One answer is, "To insure health." But at what level? One answer is the level the person had at the time the health insurance was issued, or better. How about better than normal, such as pain free or anxiety free? To be able to work and love? To move from 60% functioning to 80% or from 90% to 95%? In addition, for whom is the benefit targeted: individual, family, the company paying premiums, or society in general?

To insure medically usually has meant to provide the financial means by which to regain what has been lost through disease or accident. ("Indemnity" means to protect against accidents and the unforeseen.) If you are sick, health insurance provides the financial means by which to receive treatment intended to help you become well. If you are unable to work, disability insurance provides you a portion of the income you lose as a consequence of not being able to work. If your house is damaged, homeowners insurance provides the financial means to replace what is lost.

The meaning of insurance has been expanded on several fronts. Some insurance companies have paid for cosmetic surgery for people whose only "accident" was being born with an unsightly nose. Should such payments continue? Should insurance companies pay for clients who simply like to talk to their therapists, because they enjoy their company? Plastic surgery and "companion" psychotherapy do have helpful and cost-effective roles under some circumstances.

Therapists and clients, providers, and the public need to decide what they think is best; otherwise, the support for psychotherapy will erode as cost containment takes its toll on psychotherapy for needy clients. Will chronic schizophrenics receive the support that seems to help them (Hogarty et al., 1991)? Will clients with recurrent depression find the regular psychotherapy that seems to help prevent relapse (Frank et al., 1990)?

The vaguely defined concept of "medical necessity" needs attention. The phrase comes to mean whatever the definer wants it to mean. For profit-oriented organizations driven by cost savings, the scope of "medical necessity" continues to shrink. The rock-bottom limit has something to do with the capacity to regain daily functioning. Few will argue the necessity of putting a cast on a broken leg, removing an inflamed appendix, or providing antibiotics for pneumonia, but there is less consensus about the medical necessity of psychotherapy for many psychological problems.

*Which **people** with what kinds of **problems** in which **settings** should receive what **psychotherapy** from which **therapists**?* The answer to this question requires much thought. Ultimately, like most laws and policies, the answer will reflect the values of those most influential in defining rules, laws, and policies. The values embraced by psychotherapy are easily stated:

1. Belief in the individual's ability to assume responsibility to respond to stressful circumstances.
2. Respect for the psychological and emotional life of others.
3. Encouragement of the resolution of conflict through discussion.

Will the policies directing the place of psychotherapy in American health care support the continuation of these values?

Policies are born in two ways. First, they may evolve from the ground up, from small decisions that aggregate into rules that govern organizational and individual behavior. In the specific example of psychotherapy, policy is being directed by MCOs that are trying to cut costs by restricting access. In its most money-saving form, MCO policy toward psychotherapy would eliminate it as "cosmetic, discretionary, and medically unnecessary." If all MCOs are able to create policy on their own without input from consumers, providers, and governments, then this cost-savings objective would determine de facto policy. Second, policies also evolve from governmental and political efforts to guide resources according to defined goals. If the values contained within psychotherapy are embraced by the general public and psychotherapy is perceived by government and employers as useful, then quality will take a firm place in policy development.

Which People?

Who is potentially eligible to become a psychotherapy client? Those who have a payer behind them. A review of the payers becomes a necessary part of the answer to the question posed above. Many payers fear that discretionary use will encourage high utilization and high costs. Unknown to most casual observers is the fact that between 1948 and 1989, in a variety of clinical settings, the median number of sessions has held steady at 3-13, usually hovering between 4 and 8 (Garfield, 1994). Utilization review should be triggered automatically for any sessions frequency over 20.

The major payers cover the following number of lives.

Employees:	65 million (half of those employed are covered by health insurance)
Medicare:	37 million
Medicaid:	35 million
CHAMPUS:	5 million
Prisoners:	1 million
Uninsured:	28 million, of whom 8% or 2.2 million earned $50,000 or more in 1993 (Davis et al., 1995).

From a U.S. psychotherapy policy perspective, not all persons should be eligible for psychotherapy benefits. For example, individuals with sufficient income should pay their own costs for specific minor problems but should be covered for major problems. Many individuals will have sufficient incomes to permit them the option to enter psychotherapy without a third-party payer. People spend many thousands of dollars on laser surgery for wrinkles, dietary supplements, and exercise programs. The public also seems, however, to highly value love, good interpersonal relationships, self-acceptance, and the ability to respond smoothly to stress and conflict.

The cost of four sessions could be equivalent to a weekend vacation or a dinner with friends in an expensive restaurant. The benefits are likely to be longer lasting. If psychotherapists market together, market share will be enhanced. Market forces and public policy decisions will shape the future identity of psychotherapy clients.

Which Settings?

The needs and wishes of inner-city inhabitants can differ significantly from those of suburban dwellers. Inner-city residents may wish to disregard domestic violence as a problem, whereas middle-class suburbanites may wish to attack the problem directly. People living in large coastal cities can aspire to psychological endpoints different from those in the middle of the country.

Clients with chronic medical diseases are at greater risk for psychological problems because of the added stress of the disease to already burdened lives. Should psychotherapists appear regularly in the lives of people with these illnesses because evidence suggests a prolongation of life and improvement in quality of life in some diseases (Fawzy et al., 1990; Spiegel et al., 1989)?

The workplace is increasingly understood as a source of satisfaction as well as stress-induced difficulties. Employee assistance programs have provided an entrance into these domains. Psychotherapy is becoming a regular part of workplace support. Similarly, psychotherapy can function as part of the overall services offered in elementary schools, high schools, colleges, and graduate schools.

Simply because one has a payer behind him or her does not necessarily make that person a client for psychotherapy. If a gatekeeper is required for a person to become a client, persons seeking psychotherapy may be required to enter a primary care clinic before being admitted to clienthood. A person who is traveling or living outside the geographical network may be eligible to see a therapist but cannot do so because distance prohibits an appointment. Some plans place specialty services at such a distance from a potential client's residence that psychotherapy contact is prohibited.

What Problems?

What problems do the basic benefit package permit to be treated by psychotherapy? Most HMOs do not include sexual dysfunction as a problem to be covered in the benefit design, although there is excellent evidence that sexual dysfunction can be responsive to psychotherapeutic intervention. Some argue that only major psychiatric problems that have reasonable evidence for a biological/genetic basis—such as schizophrenia, manic-depressive illness, major depression, obsessive-compulsive disorder, and panic disorder—be included in benefit designs. Personal problems that disrupt marriages and families but do not fit into neat diagnostic categories must also find their ways more easily into the consulting room because early prevention can decrease long-term costs.

Perhaps the most direct way to answer this question involves determining the outcomes that are most important to the payers and potential clients and then estimating in the aggregate the total costs for these desired outcomes.

What Therapies and How Many Sessions?

The debates about the relevance of experimentally validated therapies (Goldfried & Wolfe, 1996) to clinical practice will continue, but practice guidelines will be implemented in part under the direction of research findings. More crucial to cost containment than "brand name" of a therapy is the question "How many sessions is enough?"

> The question "how much is enough?" is ultimately intertwined with the question "How much should we pay for it?" If one looks at payment for outpatient psychotherapy as one of the many components of the healthcare dollar, the question becomes "What percentage of the dollar should be spent on this treatment?" How this question is answered depends, in turn, on issues of proven effectiveness, cost offset of other medical services, consumer preference, and in some relative valuing of all health-related interventions. (Howard & O'Mahoney, 1996)

Psychotherapy research has demonstrated that more therapy produces better results than less therapy when one considers all clients entering therapy. Clearly, some clients benefit substantially from a few sessions, some become worse (5%), and many do not profit from therapies that go on for years (Lambert, 1996). When using global outcome assessments, however, treatment response tends to "flatten out" perhaps around 26 sessions; each incremental session adds less to change than earlier sessions. From a financial perspective, the price of each additional session buys less change than early in treatment (Howard et al., 1986).[5]

Which Therapists?

Profiles of therapist effectiveness will show that some therapists are better for some problems with certain clients than are others. These profiles can be used to improve cost-effectiveness and quality. Such profiles need to be implemented ethically to avoid destroying careers unnecessarily.

Policy decisions should include the development of a cadre of generalist therapists to handle the easier problems in systematic ways. There then should be a group of therapists who are highly specialized. Policy should define when it is more cost-effective to have one person administer both medications and psychotherapy and when it is more cost- and quality-effective to split these functions (Goldman, 1996). Policymakers need to consider when it might be more effective to match clients by gender, ethnic background, and religious affiliations. The distribution of individual, group, couple, and family therapy programs requires careful weighing of outcomes. Group therapy has a clear opportunity to demonstrate its promise of cost-effectiveness.

NOTES

1. Manuals, defined as descriptions in sufficient detail to allow a trained clinician to replicate the treatment, have been shown to be experimentally validated treatments (EVTs) in the following diagnostic categories:

> Bulimia: cognitive behavioral and interpersonal
> Chronic headache: behavioral
> Chronic pain: cognitive behavioral
> Chronic mental illness: token economies
> Depression: cognitive, interpersonal
> Discordant couples: behavior therapy
> Enuresis: behavioral
> Generalized anxiety disorder: anxiety management, cognitive behavior
> Obsessive-compulsive disorder: behavioral
> Panic disorder: cognitive
> Post-traumatic stress disorder: cognitive behavior
> Social phobia: cognitive behavioral group therapy
> Specific phobia: systematic desensitization, exposure therapy
> (Sanderson & Woody, 1995)

In the psychotherapeutic treatment of depression in older adults, research evidence has demonstrated the efficacy of CBT and brief psychodynamic (including interpersonal) therapy compared to spontaneous remission. Treatment effects were described as durable. In addition to demonstrating efficacy, the author of the review urges readers to understand that age does not predict decreasing responsiveness to psychotherapy and, in fact, older people are just as responsive as those in other age groups (Niederebe, 1996).

Gabbard and Lazar (1997) reviewed the research literature describing several other areas of note:

> Metastatic breast cancer clients participating in a year of weekly group psychotherapy showed reduced anxiety, nausea, fatigue, and pain; improved coping; and double the survival of a control group. The improved prognosis was not achieved with brief therapy (Spiegel, Bloom, Kraemer, & Gottheil, 1989).

Malignant melanoma clients demonstrated an enhanced immune response after 6 weeks of group psychotherapy. The improved immune response correlated with reduction in depression and anxiety (Fawzy, Elashoff, Norton, Cousins, & Fawzy, 1990). In addition, the treated clients had less recurrence and improved survival compared to the control group (Fawzy et al., 1993).

In a study of 184 clients with a diagnosis of multiple personality disorder, clients participated in twice-weekly psychotherapy for 30 months. More than 80% achieved a high level of stabilization and remained well during the 2- to 10-year follow-up (Kluft & Kluft, 1988). Another study suggested that spontaneous remission of multiplicity without definitive psychotherapy does not occur (Kluft, 1985).

Mortality among clients with anorexia nervosa who received intensive, specialized psychotherapeutic care was one-fifth that of clients who received brief general medical care (Crisp, 1992).

From the public's perspective, the strong support for psychotherapy described in *Consumer Reports* ("Mental Health: Does Therapy Work?," 1995) provides yet more evidence to support the practice of psychotherapy because the study was done in the real world of real clients outside research domains. The magazine's researchers surveyed 4,000 readers of *Consumer Reports* and found that the majority were highly satisfied with the help they had received. The article bemoaned the fact that many Americans do not have the opportunity to receive this helpful treatment. It found, as have others, that more therapy usually meant more benefit, in this way striking a blow against rigid brief therapy. The study has received massive criticism by psychotherapy researchers. Each of its conclusions has been challenged and its methodological weakness amplified (Jacobson & Christensen, 1996). How can the combination of pharmacotherapy and psychotherapy be equivalent to psychotherapy alone (Hollon, 1996)? For the research-based public image of psychotherapy, the *Consumer Reports* survey strengthens the value of psychotherapy in the public mind.

2. Jones and Vischi (1979) reviewed the literature of 25 studies that examined whether mental health intervention reduced subsequent medical care utilization. The median reduction for mental illness intervention was 20% and for alcohol abuse 40%. These studies took place in staff model HMOs utilizing outpatient psychotherapy. In reviewing these and other studies, there was little agreement about what period of time to use as baseline for utilization and then how far to extend the postintervention time. The reduction in utilization may increase as time after psychotherapy increases (Jameson, Shuman, & Young, 1978). The Jameson and colleagues (1978) study also showed a 30% drop in total cost per client per month for the treated group, with the biggest reduction occurring among the 21% of the treated group who were identified as high utilizers of medical care.

Mental health interventions for clients with chronic medical conditions such as ischemic heart disease, hypertension, diabetes, and pulmonary problems have reduced total medical care costs (e.g., Pallak, Cummings, Dorken, & Henke, 1994; Schlesinger, Mumford, & Glass, 1983). Many other studies have demonstrated that mental health interventions can reduce medical costs. Some managed care companies seem to be recognizing this fact and are responding by incorporating mental health services for medically ill clients. In addition, many clients visiting their primary care physicians have no diagnosable medical problem but instead are experiencing some forms of anxiety and/or depression. "60% of physician visits that the nation's prototype HMO found were primarily responding to somaticized stress rather than physical disease" (Pallak et al., 1994). Many such clients appear to be more cost-effectively served by behavioral health providers.

In 1992, 20% of medical costs went for unnecessary services and procedures (Sobel, 1994). Studies demonstrated improved outcomes with simple inexpensive procedures including client education through videos, classes, and/or individual counseling sessions; encouraging clients to play an active role in their own health care; stress management techniques; and organized tender loving care. Nearly one-third of clients visiting doctors develop bodily symptoms as an expression of psychological distress. Another one-third have medical conditions that result from behavioral choices such as smoking, alcohol and drug abuse, or a poor diet. Another one-third with chronic medical diseases such as arthritis and heart failure have their course of illness influenced by their mood, coping skills, and social support (Pallak et al., 1994).

3. Supporters of legislation restricting psychotherapy seem to wish only to force their views of the world onto their practice-based colleagues without recognizing the methodological limitations of their conclusions.

First, respected researchers in perhaps the most respected psychotherapy research volume, *Handbook of Psychotherapy and Behavior Change* (Bergin & Garfield, 1994), conclude that common factors across the therapies are more critical to outcome than the specific techniques that characterize different EVTs. Technique has a place but not the reified positions insisted on by different schools (Lambert & Bergin, 1994).

Second, diagnosis plays very different roles in research versus practice. In research, the main function of diagnosis is to allow the study to be replicated with similar clients treated according to the standard protocol; reliability is more central than validity because of the need for replication. In practice, diagnosis is intended as a blueprint for action. Here validity is primary; in the absence of a valid diagnosis, the label may simply be used to qualify for managed care or insurance reimbursement. Researchers attempt to avoid Type I errors, the inclusion of those without the desired diagnosis in the study. Clinicians strive to avoid Type II errors, exclusion or failure to make the diagnosis in clients who actually have the disorder. Hence, the researcher uses very rigid criteria and the clinician uses fairly loose criteria (Fensterheim & Raw, 1996).

Third, research findings have had notorious difficulty generalizing to the real world of practice (Goldfried & Wolfe, 1996; McIntyre, Zarin, & Pincus, 1996). Most research has focused on symptom change in homogeneous client groups. Many clients coming for help do not fit the homogeneous criteria of research protocols. They are interested not only in symptom relief but also in functioning more capably in their social and work relationships. Only recently have psychotherapy researchers (and pharmacotherapy researchers) included quality of life and functioning as outcome measures. Furthermore, if the client does not fit research criteria for a study demonstrating the effectiveness of an EVT, is the client then not to be treated in this way even if the client fits some of the research admission criteria?

Fourth, by stifling innovation, EVT supporters are claiming that what we know about psychotherapy currently is sufficient. Ideas for EVTs came from clinician ingenuity and careful observation. Forcing clinicians into manualized treatment formats would throw the field back to orthodoxy. Clinicians and researchers (Barlow, 1996; Goldfried & Wolfe, 1996) are attempting to reach out to each other, but rigid research-based conclusions, especially from researchers who are not in clinical practice, will further confuse our concepts of psychotherapy practice.

4. One of the weaknesses of the psychotherapy oversight function in many states derives from the existence of individual boards for individual professions. Prior to 1988, only two mental health professions were regulated in Colorado: psychologists and social workers. In 1987, separate boards were created to oversee the regulatory efforts of counselors as well as marriage and family therapists; however, none of the four boards was authorized to hear and determine the validity of complaints against practitioners. Instead, these responsibilities were granted to the Grievance Board. Psychology and social work had been unaggressive in pursuing disciplinary actions. Psychology had brought only 10 actions in 26 years, and the Social Work Board pursued only 3 in its 12-year history. There was a perceived lack of willingness to bring action against a colleague. In addition, legislators recognized a need to police unlicensed psychotherapists. They created a Grievance Board to oversee all the psychotherapists in the state. The board is composed of four public members and one member of each of the licensed professions. The membership is increased by three members of the profession of anyone for whom disciplinary action is being considered. The board also keeps an annually updated record of all licensed and unlicensed psychotherapists including name, address, education, therapeutic orientation/methodology, and years of experience in each specialty area.

During the period 1988-1994, more than 1,000 complaints against about 800 therapists were filed with the Grievance Board, an average of about 145 per year. About 20% (228) were not dismissed and resulted in a hearing or investigation to determine the validity of the allegations. From these cases, 133 disciplinary actions were taken, including injunctions and sanctions (restriction of practice). Fewer than 5% of psychotherapists had actions taken against them during this period. If it were assumed that each therapist saw only 15 clients in a 1-year period, a very conservative estimate, the ratio of actions taken to clients seen would be about 2 per 1,000 for psychologists and less for other professions (Schmitt, 1995).

The empowering of a new board composed of professionals outside that of the practitioner under investigation may have added to the number of disciplinary actions taken, in addition to the accompanying tightening of regulations. These data suggest that much work needs to be done in other states to develop bureaucracies that address the problem of incompetent and unethical therapists.

5. The fundamental question for policymakers who must help decide how to spend limited funds is this: What do we want for our money? Once a set of desired outcomes is determined, the next question involves how to measure the outcome in a systematic way. If, for example, we are simply seeking client satisfaction with treatment, improvement is likely to be high because consumers inflate this rating beyond more objective criteria. If the desired endpoint is symptom reduction, then a symptom checklist will suffice. If the more expensive goals of improved interpersonal relationships and work functioning become the target in addition to symptom reduction, then a different scale would be required, as well as greater investment. If we are looking for "just enough treatment" to prevent relapse, then follow-up studies would be required to determine how much would be necessary for the next client matching the algorithm established by the follow-up studies.

Ideally, naturalistic and research findings from a data bank could be formed into an outcome expectancy table into which initial data about each client and subsequent response to ongoing treatment could be placed as a means of predicting this client's dose-response curve (number of sessions needed to achieve specified results). Initial values such as symptom severity, strength of the social network, chronicity, and readiness to change could be used to predict the number of sessions required at the beginning of treatment. After five sessions, for example, the degree of improvement and the strength of the working alliance could be matched to data in the table, which would suggest the next number of sessions necessary for positive outcome. Cost-containment policies then could be implemented to determine whether the next number of required sessions should be allotted.

The general problem of defining how much is enough includes the question "For whom is therapy going to be ineffective?" and the related question of "Who may be harmed?" Quicker terminations could result from a ready answer to these questions. Instead, therapists tend to keep trying in the face of poor progress. Cost containment is pushing therapists (and clients) to recognize the limits of their ability to use psychotherapy profitably.

7

Participation in Systems
Outside Psychotherapy

Get out of your office! Therapists will find several intersecting systems that can assist them in client care and economic survival: medical groups, self-help groups, and politics.

FIT BEHAVIORAL HEALTH AND
MEDICINE/SURGERY TOGETHER

The highest percentage of cost-containing money is paid for the care of the medically ill. Perhaps 75% of each dollar allocated for diagnosis and treatment is designated for medical/surgical costs, which include diagnostic testing, hospitalizations, and treatment. The rest is distributed to administration, pharmacy, home health care, and mental health. These latter three tend to be managed separately by a company or group different from those managing medical/surgical care. They are "carved out" from general management. Whether it is in the best interests of clients and systems to have mental health *carved in* or *carved out* remains a question for debate and research.

Arguments in favor of carve outs emphasize the uniqueness of mental health treatment as compared to medical/surgical treatment. As managed care evolved, MCOs recognized that medical or surgical nurses acting as utilization reviewers had little experience in evaluating the necessity of mental health treatments. Furthermore, managers of the major medical aspects of managed care health plans tended to ignore mental health or minimize its importance. The details of mental health plan administration, however, rivaled the details of the medical/surgical plans. MCOs therefore asked specialty organizations familiar with borderline personalities, drug abuse, suicidal threats, and organic brain syndromes to help in managing costs, quality, and appropriateness of mental health care. These specialty organizations then carried much of the financial risk.

From the perspective of MCOs and payers, carve outs allowed them to shift financial risk away from general medicine. Neither the MCO nor the payer was confident of effective management within their existing structures.

If behavioral health is carved in, on the other hand, then the MCO manages all care from a single pool of money. The general medicine administrators will have the opportunity to treat mental health in the same way they treat other specialties in medicine and surgery, such as dermatology and orthopedics. Each could "subcapitate," which means that the per member per month capitation rate is divided into parts directly related to the client demands for these services. The bias against and misunderstanding of mental illness, however, are likely to influence the amount of the subcapitation allocated to mental health. If history from indemnity insurance benefit packages is any indicator, mental health treatment is likely to receive a disproportionately reduced share when carved in. Carved out management of mental health services guarantees a separate budget so that general medicine does not have the opportunity to take from mental health funding. A separate carved out budget makes sure a fixed amount of money is spent on mental health. One of the problems for carved out systems involves the complex decision about how to provide incentives for primary care physicians to treat mental illness when the easiest approach would be to refer to a mental health specialist who, by being carved out, is paid from a separate pool of money (Frank et al., 1995).

Advocates of carving in praise the integration of mind and body implied by including mental health treatment as part of the entire package of health care. It may be time for allopathic medicine to recognize the need for treatment systems that take into consideration the complex web of interactions between psyche and soma (Pope, 1997).

Carve in supporters hope that by functioning within the general medicine capitation, mental health professionals will work closely with primary care physicians and specialists to find ways to reduce the costs associated with perhaps 15-35% of clients whose major problems can be settled by behavioral health interventions. As described in the previous chapter, there is much evidence to support the belief that psychotherapy and other mental health interventions can provide cost savings. Unfortunately for the mental health professions, although there is no need to prove that treatment of pneumonia provides a cost offset, the treatment of depression requires statistical rather than face-valid evidence.

To integrate behavioral health with general medicine requires the continuing development of various pathways to which mental health technology can be applied, with continuing assessment of its cost-benefit. These pathways could include (a) direct information and decision support for clients *before* they seek treatment, (b) stress reduction through the relaxation response and biofeedback, (c) lifestyle improvements (e.g., chain smoking, alcohol use, diet, and exercise habits), (d) improved social support (because supportive relationships insulate against disease), (e) screening for undiagnosed psychiatric disorders (that can lead to many fruitless nonpsychiatric clinician visits), and (f) identification of somatization (because many clients seem to overly interpret physical sensations as symptoms of disease, leading to frequent medical office visits) (Friedman, Sobel, Myers, Caudhill, & Benson, 1995).

SELF-HELP GROUPS

One of the purposes of psychotherapy may be to eliminate the need for itself. The successes of self-help books, mutual support groups and, possibly, trained paraprofessionals suggest that increasingly more psychotherapeutic services may be taking place among nonprofessionals. Some estimates suggest that more than 2,000 self-help books are published in this country annually. Others suggest that there are 750,000 self-help and mutual help groups in the United States with about 15 million members (Christensen & Jacobson, 1994). Efficient and effective providers incorporate the less expensive procedures from self-help books, self-help groups, and network on-line therapy groups to achieve results without having to pay the more expensive professionals. Effective behavioral health organizations also need to consider organizing peer counseling (Jackins, 1978) to help members help each other inexpensively. Therapists who do not incorporate successful self-help groups into their treatment plans are likely not to compete as successfully as those organizations and individual therapists that do.

College professors with no clinical experience or training and who had reputations for being warm and trustworthy were compared with psychotherapists who had an average of 23 years of experience. College students were randomly assigned to these two therapist groups with no difference in outcome, although both treatments were more effective than the control group (Strupp & Hadley, 1979). The study does not suggest that psychotherapy training is unimportant but instead that under proper conditions (e.g., careful monitoring by the research staff), highly motivated and psychologically minded clients can have successful encounters with empathic, warm, and respectful nonprofessionals (Strupp, 1997).

These data suggest that professional psychotherapists could be participating in a decreasing percentage of psychotherapeutic encounters as the general population absorbs the fruits of psychotherapeutic research and experience. Professionals may become consultants for the difficult clients who cannot be helped in the more cost-efficient self-help and group methods. The fact that 30% of Americans are likely to qualify for one or more diagnoses for mental illness sometime in their lives suggests that professionals will not and cannot reach them all. Therapists will need to anticipate variations in practice patterns that take these self-help innovations into consideration (Christensen & Jacobson, 1994).

Effective therapists will motivate their clients to associate closely with self-help groups: Alcoholics Anonymous (AA), Agoraphobics in Motion; depression and manic-depression groups, and incest and rape survivors groups are all out there to help. The American Self-Help Clearinghouse has information on regional self-help clearinghouses.[1] Self-help groups are not panaceas and in some cases actually make disorders worse (e.g., panic disorders increase for some clients who survive by not thinking about their attacks and then go to a panic group; alcoholics in AA find some attendees only looking for drinking buddies). Nevertheless, these groups survive because they help a great many people.

POLITICAL ACTIONS TO CONSIDER

Power yields only to power. Although cost-containment efforts will not recede, their excesses and biases against mental health treatment can be altered. Therapists must now study the political landscape in which they are functioning to bring about necessary corrections in the path of the cost-containment juggernaut for the benefit of psychotherapy practice and their clients. Political action requires the mobilization of large numbers of people focused in a unified direction who bring their concerns directly to decision makers. The strongest coalitions will include representatives of all the psychotherapy professions, clients, former clients and their families, and organized friends of the cause (including employer groups and national organizations whose interests might overlap). The targets are not only governments (federal, state, and local) but also private payers like businesses and educational institutions, the media, and managed care companies themselves. Large numbers of consumer-provider groups attracting media attention can attenuate excesses by managed care companies.

For example, in the mid-1990s, MCOs tried to force postpartum women to go home within 24 hours of delivering their babies. A media outcry embarrassed legislators into passing laws against this practice.

To take political action requires several coordinated elements. The scientific database demonstrating efficacy coupled with the development of a constituency supporting the value of psychotherapy can lead to a coherent plan defining the role of psychotherapy in the health care system. Various political actions include new legislation supporting psychotherapy within parity for mental health, attacks on laws that impair the practice of medicine and psychotherapy, consideration of the value of universal health care and psychotherapy, and campaigns to better inform consumers about the value of psychotherapy and their potential power in new funding schemes. By joining forces with physicians, allied health professionals, community supporters, and consumer groups for mutually beneficial purposes, the psychotherapy constituency can effectively exert its influence in the political arena.

Propose New Legislation

In 1996, the U.S. Congress and the president approved legislation that prevents health benefit plans that cover mental illness from having lower annual and lifetime limits for coverage of mental illness than for coverage of other illnesses. This legislation represents a major step toward parity between mental health benefits and general medicine benefits. This legislation was produced by massive, persistent lobbying by consumers, professionals, and key senators and representatives. Unlike earlier proposed legislation, which would have required insurers with mental health plans to apply the same rules to deductibles, copayments, and visit limits for mental health care as all other health care, this compromised legislation left insurers free to manage the benefit as they wished subject only to generally equal upper limits. The compromise excluded substance abuse treatment. The plan has loopholes (e.g., if the benefit plan eliminates mental health coverage, then it is not covered by the law); nevertheless, it may have opened the door to stronger parity initiatives. The more psychotherapists who get behind these initiatives, the greater the likelihood of passage.

Modify Existing Laws

Know the meaning of ERISA. The Employee Retirement Income Security Act, well-meaning legislation filling more than 400 pages, protects many large employers from being sued by clients because of limited managed care coverage that leads to poor treatment. Keep in mind the need to circumvent or reduce the power of this law. Many companies scurry to hide behind ERISA protection.[2]

Know the limits imposed by antitrust laws. If a group of providers wants to become a legal entity to compete together in the new health care marketplace, they should consider limits imposed by federal antitrust laws. These laws make provider sponsored networks more difficult to create.

If, for example, a group of hospitals in an area agrees to a minimum rate that they will accept, they can be accused of violating antitrust laws as anticompetitive collusion. In fact, any integrated delivery system in a marketplace, including hospitals and group practices, could be accused of antitrust violations. For example, current federal regulations governing Medicare and Medicaid penalize physicians who receive "kickbacks" from providers for referrals (for example, a primary care physician receiving payment for referring clients to a group of psychotherapists). Would a primary care physician who is part of a provider-owned HMO be guilty of fraud for referring to a psychotherapist within his own network? After all, the physician has an economic interest in the referral. Antitrust and referral regulations offer MCO business entrepreneurs a significant advantage over providers (Stone, 1995). Individuals and small groups are being dwarfed by the size and increasing competitive advantage being grabbed by large business and insurance groups that advertise themselves as providers when all they do is organize provider groups and hospitals. These complex laws preventing providers from organizing themselves must be openly dissected and transformed if physicians and psychotherapists are to avoid being completely subsumed under business interests whose primary concern is their own profits.[3]

Universal Health Care?

If physicians, politicians, and the general public ever decide that adequate health care is not a commodity to be sold on the open market, but rather a right, then we may see movement toward a government-run health care program. The private system currently being created likely will be organized by a few companies with many efficiencies built into them. The trouble will be the demand for profit continuously required by profit-making organizations responsible to their shareholders. Some profit is necessary to continue to expand through research and acquisitions. Excess profit becomes money taken away from those who might otherwise receive care.

Canada has 10% of the U.S. population, spread over 10 provinces and two territories. Its federal government mandated that all citizen be provided a medical care safety net. Canada's single-payer system began in 1945, when the Liberal party fostered the development of the full range of health services. Although faced with many problems (e.g., long waiting lists for angiograms and cardiac surgery), a majority of Canadians like the system.[4] Should the United States adopt a similar system?

Inform Consumers

Physicians, psychotherapists, and health care consumers recognize the need for laws that require clear explanations of what the plan covers, its restrictions, how to obtain prior authorization for desired services (asking a company representative for permission to receive the service), and whether or not there are financial incentives for providers to limit their services. In addition, utilization review needs to include standards of "medical necessity," with these standards made public. Necessary laws have been passed or are being considered in various states to require that plans offer explanations for rejecting or terminating providers, rather than terminating "without cause," and that credentialing criteria be clearly defined and disclosed (adapted from Sharfstein, 1994).

Consumers and therapists need to realize that business pays for health insurance from money that previously would have gone directly to the individual employee's salary. The current accepted standard that business pays is not the only alternative. "Tax equity" and medical savings accounts, for example, promote individual responsibility in health care decision making. Each encourages individual responsibility for health care decisions.

Tax law and false impressions impel employees to choose employer-sponsored managed care plans. Plans bought through the employer receive unlimited tax deductibility. Currently, individuals buy personal insurance with after-tax dollars. Employees also believe that the employer is paying part of the premium when, in fact, that premium payment simply results in lower salaries and wages.

If consumers were required to pay closer attention to the costs of their health care, then they would be better shoppers and more responsible for their decisions. The simple process of raising or lowering co-payments currently influences decisions consumer-clients make, but "tax equity" and medical savings accounts (MSAs) offer two other alternatives that place increasingly more weight on individual responsibility.

The concept of "tax equity" negates the current HMO system for business employees by requiring that employees have the option of taking the money paid by the company and the employee for HMO premiums directly, as part of salary or wages. The employee could then use this money to purchase his or her own health insurance. The premium paid by the employer is not taxable, so "tax equity" would permit the employee to pay for health insurance premiums as a tax deductible expense or, better yet, as a tax credit (coming directly off the total tax paid). The difference between what the employee spends on health insurance and what the combined employee-business total had been becomes a profit (or loss) for the employee.

To help pay the out-of-pocket costs that could accrue from relatively minor medical problems, the federal government could create medical savings plans. These plans would function like Individual Retirement Accounts (IRAs) in that each employee could put after-tax (or even pre-tax) dollars into an investment plan, the earnings of which would be tax free until the money was spent. The money could be spent only for medical expenses, with several exceptions. In other words, tax-deferred investments would pay for the medical expenses that would otherwise be paid by the employer-sponsored plan and also could be used for medical expenses after termination of employment, should funds remain in the account. Such a system could ideally return health care to where it started: between provider and client (after Stock, 1995).

These proposals assume that individuals will make sound decisions. Any such individually oriented plan must take into account the immense amount of money that federal and state governments have already paid for the health consequences to individuals who have refused to wear seat belts, drive while drunk, smoke excessively without seeking help, eat poorly, and/or fail to exercise. The acceptance of individual responsibility has social consequences that would have to be woven into any rational plan. Healthy employees might choose very limited coverage and use the money for other purposes. Such expenditures would reduce the money in the risk pools for others who are or would be less fortunate. Society would be left with the problem of dealing with people who selected minimal insurance coverage, believing they were immune to misfortune, who then became severely ill but did not have sufficient coverage.

Reinventing your political self accompanies the reinvention of your professional self, as described in the next chapter.

NOTES

1. As of September 1997, this organization could be reached at 973-625-3037 or 800-367-6274, fax 973-625-8848.

2. The meaning of the acronym ERISA deserves the attention of all providers in managed care systems. In attempting to understand it, therapists are required to develop a basic understanding of the American legal system and the lawyers and businessmen who exploit it.

ERISA shifted regulation of health care from state governments to businesses themselves. ERISA was intended to impose uniform federal standards on employee benefits. All health plans covered under ERISA had to conform to the federal statute. No state regulations could be superimposed. In other words, ERISA preempts state laws in those instances in which it applies.

Unfortunately for providers of health care, the statute contains language that prevents individual clients from suing ERISA protected plans. In other words, if a client was denied treatment and suffered as a consequence of the lack of treatment, he could not sue the MCO or the employer who had hired the MCO for pain and suffering and punitive damages as is usual in malpractice cases. He could only recover from them court costs and costs of any medical procedures that should have been followed. Who then is more liable? Who is vulnerable to suit for punitive damages? The provider.

As stated in ERISA, a participant and/or beneficiary is permitted to initiate civil actions "to recover benefits due him under the terms of his plan, to enforce his rights under the terms of the plan, or to clarify his rights to future benefits under the terms of the plan" (Employee Retirement Income Security Act of 1974, 1974). The statute also permits courts to award reasonable attorney fees and costs to either party. ERISA does not, however, permit compensatory or punitive damages (Touse, 1993).

Although morally and ethically repugnant, this well-intended law has enhanced the strength of MCOs to disregard the needs of providers and clients. MCOs are protected. Providers and hospitals appear vulnerable, no matter what the ERISA protected MCOs do. Perhaps this situation is not quite so stark. As the public and professionals become clearly aware of the power of the ERISA shield, it may be possible to enact legislation to counter its tremendous effects.

3. Some hope for reversal of this legislated competitive advantage to MCOs may be arising from coalescing legal precedents. For example, the town of Joplin, Missouri, had two competing hospitals. The two hospitals decided to merge their operations. (If not, one of them would have failed. They just did not know which one.) Blue Cross decided that this was antitrust collusion because these two hospitals then could dominate the Joplin market, where there were no other hospitals. Blue Cross lawyers brought the hospitals to court, arguing that the two hospitals were creating a monopoly in the town. (Blue Cross wanted them to compete against each other. If they competed against each other, each would need to ratchet down prices to keep market share. Blue Cross, as the MCO, would have made more money because it would be able to pay lower rates.)

The antitrust laws required that the hospitals have no monopoly in the area. The problem became defining the area in which the hospitals were operating. The hospitals argued that their service area extended 100 miles from town, and therefore competition with neighboring hospitals continued to exist. Blue Cross argued that the service area was only 5 miles from town. In late 1995, the courts decided in favor of the hospitals.

Court decisions do not usually become law, but they can establish precedents for future similar cases. In many instances, providers with greater numbers will be battling employers, insurers, and MCOs with larger cash reserves. The checkerboard results of these court proceedings will help to shape the health delivery system of the near future by defining how easily provider-sponsored networks can form and operate.

4. The federal contribution for Canadian health care was set at a maximum of 60% of the established cost of a service; the other 40% was contributed by each province. By 1972, all Canadian provinces had universal coverage with unimpeded access and portability to any Canadian location. Only psychiatrists, primary care physicians, and psychiatric nurses could be reimbursed for mental health services. Other psychotherapists could not participate, although they could be paid out-of-pocket.

The plan began essentially unmanaged. It placed no limits on client demands for service or, initially, on physician fees, use of laboratory tests, or drug prescriptions programs. The result was overemphasis on inpatient care and insufficient chronic care. Eventually, the provinces initiated cost-containment strategies by putting caps on physician income and requiring repayment of any earnings above the cap. The percentage of Gross Domestic Product (GDP) paid for medical care nevertheless has gone from 7% in 1971 to 10% in 1993. As client numbers began to dwindle, primary care physicians increased their billings for psychotherapy so that they were receiving psychotherapy payments at a rate only 8% below that of psychiatrists who were actively billing for psychotherapy as well (Gold, 1996).

Physician strikes did little to change the system in favor of physicians' demands. One strike sought government subsidies for private insurance as well as the public one; another wanted the reinstatement of extra billing of clients beyond the government-set price.

Canada's system requires that U.S. specialized treatments be right across the border for cases the Canadian system does not handle quickly enough or for which it has not developed the necessary ultraspecialization. Other border crossings are taking place as Canadian government officials absorb the apparent successes of managed care in the United States. The federal government mandated in 1994 that its contribution to health and related programs be reduced by 42%. This impending financial catastrophe requires that provinces continue to increase the amount of money they contribute to maintain current provisions of the original legislation mandating access and no cost to the client. Some provinces are again proposing a two-tiered system in which clients may pay private physicians from their own pockets or from private insurance. As the downsizing takes place, Canadian hospitals are closing and Canadian physicians are leaving the country, but the appropriate continua of care have not been installed. Client care suffers. Medical school class sizes are being reduced. Foreign-trained physicians are being excluded. Older physicians are being forced to retire early. Limits are being placed on where physicians can practice. Limits on psychotherapy are being considered, especially on the practice of primary care physicians billing for these services. Several task forces are attempting to develop a definition of psychotherapy that excludes primary care physician involvement. Despite all this turmoil, Canadians may still see a physician, receive diagnostic testing, and be hospitalized without having to worry about money. Canadians appear determined to keep some form of their single-payer system (Gold, 1996; Lesser, 1995).

8

Reinvent Yourself, Again

This chapter is aimed directly at the cognitive schemata and self-talk of individual therapists. It provides self-help for therapists to gently but directly persuade you to think (and presumably then to act) differently. The fundamental message here is keep changing: (a) Involve your clients in the new business process, (b) think like a businessperson, (c) learn how to evaluate managed care contracts, (d) join or create a group or network, (e) question the necessity of insurance companies and managed care companies, (f) use psychotherapy strategies to help yourself, (g) be flexible and diversify, and (h) use the new information technologies. Much can be done to respond to these rapidly changing times, in which the only constant is change.

INVOLVE YOUR CLIENTS IN THE PROCESS OF DEALING WITH MANAGED CARE COMPANIES

To help reduce the excesses building in MCO cost-containment efforts, help to develop scorecards for managed care companies. Include, for example, ratings of the difficulty in obtaining authorization for more sessions from a particular client's company; the glitches in its system, especially those affecting your clients, such as receiving an incorrect billing statement; deceptive benefit listings—does 20 sessions maximum imply that each person has the option of 20 sessions?; and the user-friendly nature of the treatment plan form. You can also spend a very brief portion of the therapy session discussing with your client the effects of managed care on his or her treatment.

Letters from clients to their employers complaining of current undesirable practices can provide momentum for change. Not uncommonly, the line staff of an MCO creates more barriers than the managers higher up who discuss the state of service with benefits managers of employers. Letters to the more influential managers are likely to yield better results.

Effective political movement takes place at the local level. If consumers want something, government and business respond. The remarkable growth of alternative medical practitioners like chiropractors and naturopaths illustrates this fact. Chiropractic care is reimbursed by Medicare and other federal programs, and in many states by Medicaid. All states mandate that chiropractic care be covered by workers' compensation, and six require insurers to cover acupuncture. From 1975 to 1993, the percentage of clinical chiropractic revenues derived from private insurance rose from 20% to 40%. Naturopaths, whose major distinction is the use of natural products and natural therapies, are also likely to continue to grow in numbers because the American public appears to be drawn to the use of natural remedies. Neither the growth in the number of alternative medicine practitioners nor the laws and insurance practices that facilitate their access by clients would have taken place without broad public acceptance (Cooper & Stoflet, 1996).

THINK LIKE A BUSINESSPERSON

Individual clients no longer are the primary contractors. Therapists therefore must grasp the motivation of their primary customers: Businesses and governments seek cost containment. If, for a certain business, for example, the rate of increase in health care costs between 1988 and 1993 was 15% per year, and managed care brought the rate down to 3% per year, the company would have achieved a major objective. This same business might then strive for more cost saving by gaining additional reductions from providers and/or by insisting on less profit for the MCO.

Learn the difference between profit and not-for-profit MCOs. Recognize that stockholders want profits; they are less concerned about ethics, quality, and provider livelihoods. Be wary of the differences between those companies in business for the short run and quick profits versus those in for the long run, seeking sustained profits.

Watch out if you are working for staff model HMOs because their administrators are recognizing that straight salaries reduce the incentive to work. If therapists are paid an incentive through receiving a percentage of collections, work load usually increases. Perhaps more important, companies seem to have been released from the ethical obligation to pay benefits for their employees. With a surplus of providers, HMOs (and other companies as well) are trying to fire longstanding employees and then rehire them back as consultants on a fee-for-service basis, in this way eliminating the cost of benefits. Because benefits (health insurance, retirement, disability, social security taxes) run to approximately 25% of salary, the elimination of four salaried positions and replacement by four consultant positions saves the cost of one full-time equivalent employee ($4 \times 25\% = 1$). In other words, five nonsalaried positions cost the same as four salaried positions.

LEARN HOW TO EVALUATE
MANAGED CARE CONTRACTS

Given the complexity of the contracts associated with managed care, individual providers and the groups of which they are a part face difficult decisions. The decision to enter capitated arrangements requires much knowledge about one's own financial picture because the capitated group must comprehend its own ability to serve a designated population within the financial risk corridor defined by the agreement: How can we serve this number of clients and make a profit? Legal counsel often is necessary. Consider the following questions as you evaluate managed care contracts, with special attention to capitation contracts (Hirschfelder, 1995; Pollack, 1995; Schultz, 1995).

1. How strong is the managed care system? Is it an insurance company that has diversified into managed care, or is it a non-insurance company focused primarily on managed care?

An insurance company has a distinct advantage over a non-insurance MCO because the insurance company can focus on existing clients covered by other insurance mechanisms as their initial targets to maintain market share, through a now broader product line including managed care.

An MCO with high-quality cost-management mechanisms like a data management system to monitor enrollment, resource utilization, claims processing, finance, marketing, and quality assurance teams has a higher probability of success. A network of respected providers already participating also helps.

2. What percentage of the premium dollar is allocated to client care, administration, marketing, and behavioral health? Nationally, HMOs spend 40-50% of their income on hospital care, 20-25% on physician care, 13-20% on advertising, 2-8% on catastrophic reserves (in case of major costly illness), 10-25% on administration, and 5-15% for profit or program expansion. Mature HMOs spend 35-40% on hospital care and 35-40% for primary care physicians. A newly organized HMO will spend a higher proportion on advertising and administration. The percentage allocated for behavioral health can be 3-5% of each premium dollar.

3. Is the contract exclusive, or can therapists contract with competing systems? In new managed care markets in large cities, an MCO will have trouble guaranteeing referrals; therefore, an exclusive contract would not be to a therapist's advantage. On the other hand, in mature markets, a strong MCO system may be desirable if the system has an extensive client membership in the therapist's region and is willing to limit the number of participating therapists.

4. Does the contract automatically renew each year? If it does renew automatically, some contracts allow for reimbursement modification without prior notification to the therapist. Many provider groups not only request notification of fee changes but also request provider profiling from the MCO for comparison with their own data to judge the reasons for the fee changes.

Contracts may also contain escalator clauses tying fee increases to premium increases, inflation, or some other mutually agreeable index. The first negotiation differs from subsequent renegotiation in that the provider group knows precisely what the utilization has been and where additional cost savings may be achieved. Unfortunately, a cost-saving, high-quality provider group could be at a disadvantage if the payer sees these efficiencies as an opportunity to lower costs even further by insisting on a reduction rather than an increase in fees.

5. How is "covered services" defined? Make sure the definition of covered services is in the contract you sign and not only in the contract between the MCO and the payer, because an MCO-payer contract can be modified without provider involvement. The definition of covered services should include the maximum number of visits providers are obligated under the capitation rate to provide as well as the diagnoses and other problems that are covered under the concept of "medical necessity." Other important details include explication of reimbursement amounts to providers for those clients who were authorized for treatment by the MCO by mistake because they were not actually members of the HMO. Copayments also need to be described precisely.

6. Does the system contract provide a specific definition of "medical necessity"? If the contract does not contain a clear definition of this important term, it should clearly state who will determine medical necessity criteria. An acceptable definition includes services that are "appropriate and necessary for the diagnosis and treatment of medical conditions such as Axis I diagnoses in DSM-IV."

7. What arrangements for professional coverage are required when the therapist is unavailable? Some MCOs require special arrangements for therapist absences and may levy financial penalties if a therapist circumvents referral guidelines or may require a therapist to reimburse a noncontracting provider who covers that therapist's clients.

8. How is utilization review (UR) handled? If the reviewers are not local, they may apply standards that vary from local practice standards and thereby increase therapists' noncompliance risks. If UR is subcontracted to another organization, therapists should determine whether they are covered by malpractice, because their decisions could lead to

inadequate treatment. The UR procedures should be clearly spelled out in manual form for your review.

9. What is the frequency of denial of treatment requests and appeals by the HMO? MCOs vary in the percentage of denials for treatment requests. If the rate is high, what are the reasons? The process of appeal should be clearly defined, as should which mental health professionals will be involved in the proceedings.

10. Does the contract contain a "withhold" clause in fee-for-service arrangements? The MCO retains (withholds) a percentage of the fee pending year-end evaluation of over- or underutilization. If therapist fees come out of the primary care physician's capitation allotment, primary care physicians will be reluctant to refer to behavioral providers. When the withhold is returned, mature contracts require that it be accompanied by interest. Actuarial figures should be available to providers for the population in question to determine the probability that therapists will receive their withhold.

11. Does the contract contain a "hold-harmless clause"? A hold-harmless clause can shift most contractual liability from the MCO to the therapist because the MCO is held harmless no matter what the providers do. Although restrictions such as prior authorization, utilization limitations, or restraints imposed under the guise of cost containment may impede proper treatment, under a hold-harmless clause the therapist assumes all responsibility. Such contracts are to be avoided.

12. Under what circumstances can the therapist terminate the contract? Because therapist contract terms may be tied to the client contract term (length of time contracted for covered lives membership), therapists cannot terminate until the client contract is terminated. Therapists are ethically required to notify each of their clients in case of termination by the therapist.

13. Under what circumstances can MCOs terminate contracts? A 5-year contract that can be terminated in 120 days is a 120-day contract. All contracts should have *cause* (for dropping a provider from the panel) defined as serious, unremediated provider defaults. Written no-

tice and reasonable opportunity for remedy of problems are essential provisions to termination clauses.

14. What clinical and administrative quality indicators are to be followed? Quality indicators are specific, measurable criteria that indicate good quality. Clinical indicators may include relapse/recidivism rates; appeals made by clients, families, and other providers; and adverse incidents including suicide attempts, legal problems, and harm to others. Administrative indicators may include provider access measures (including the number of telephone rings before the therapist's receptionist answers, telephone access to clinicians for clinical inquiries, and time to the initial appointment), network access measures (including provider turnover in the network, geographic proximity to covered lives, distribution of specialists for the covered members), and claims payment measures (including accuracy of billing in terms of coding and pricing as well as claims turnaround time).

15. What potential breaches of confidentiality may be contained in the contract? Some contracts insist that any and all records can become the property of the MCO, thereby completely eliminating client confidentiality. Some provision may be required in the contract to prevent the MCO from demanding information that is beyond the ability of the provider data management system to provide. For example, if your information system does not track change scores in depression rating scales, you will not be able to provide this information, although the contract may require it.

16. Are you signing the real contract? Some companies offer you a short simple contract that refers to terms and conditions described in a "provider manual." If the plan has such a manual, it may be the size of a dictionary. You may have to read it. When you sign the contract, make sure it stipulates that the contract holds the plan to the manual as it stands on the date of the signature; otherwise, the plan can amend the manual after you are already bound by the contract to follow it.

This listing provides only a sample of the many tricks business lawyers can play on you. Until therapists organize in large groups, individuals and small groups are vulnerable to dishonest, although legal, maneuvers. Therapists generally are not familiar with this culture. You can and must learn to protect yourself. Legal counsel, an additional expense, has become necessary for therapists.

A few days after the initial negotiation of the contract, a large packet of paper is likely to arrive. It may bear little resemblance to what you thought you had discussed on the phone and in meetings. The draft is likely to be one-sided (and not your side). Be suspicious if your list of obligations is several pages long and the list for the payer is less than a half a page. In the case of default on the contract, what are the contracting group's rights and what are the payer's rights? Strive to get both the list of obligations and the list of default rights about equal in length.

You may wonder if a large multistate company will negotiate the language of its standard contract. It will negotiate, because it is submitting this contract to establish a favorable position in the bargaining with you.

There are several important reasons to negotiate changes.

1. Some of the provisions of the contract may not be acceptable to you. Be prepared not to sign the contract.
2. The contract may not accurately reflect the discussions you held with the marketing staff because the marketing staff may not have communicated the complete contents of the discussions with the company lawyer who drafted the contract.
3. Initial contract negotiations set the stage for the long-term relationship—a kind of engagement stage. Are you respected in the process? Are your phone calls returned promptly? Make clear your limits and find out what provisions the payer is unwilling to change. Find out the reasons for this unwillingness to change to better define your own risk in negotiating with the payer in the future.

When the final draft of the contract is delivered, be sure to read it carefully, especially the definitions, because costs and risks often are contained in them. Make sure that everything discussed in the negotiations appears as you wanted it in the contract (Pollack, 1995).

JOIN OR CREATE A GROUP OR NETWORK

Get on panels, a task much easier to accomplish where managed care market penetration is lower. Define specific specialty areas and market yourself with brief documents describing your abilities. Even if a particular panel is closed, the MCO might be open to an offer for a therapist covering specialized areas. Although many solo practitioners will continue to fight for their own independence, obtaining managed care contracts and even becoming a panel member will be increasingly more difficult by oneself. MCOs usually prefer to have one signature by a representative of a provider group to bring many good clinicians into their panel rather than having to work out multiple contracts.

Collaborate with former competitors. There is power in numbers. Develop integrated, vertical, multispecialty systems of psychiatrists, psychologists, social workers, psychiatric nurses, certified addiction counselors, and family and marriage therapists, all in a way that will allow large groups of providers to gain leverage in the larger system and to be able to negotiate effectively with insurers, employers, general managed care companies, carve out companies, and others (Fink, 1995). EAPs as part of a multidisciplinary group can provide the opportunity to catch a client earlier in the cycle of illness, before the situation becomes too serious. It is also easier for therapists to rule out medical problems and to receive psychiatric medications when working with physicians in the same office complex, using "one-stop shopping" (Hemmersbaugh, 1995). There will continue to be resistance as practitioners strive to maintain autonomy, but the economics of cost containment are forcing most mental health practitioners into employment by government, managed care companies, institutions, group practices, and networks.

Learn the general principles of regional network development. From the individual therapist perspective, these ideally will be provider-sponsored networks (PSNs). Developing such networks requires a significant amount of energy and knowledge, as suggested by the formation of our hypothetical company, Mental Health, Inc., described in Chapter 2. The greatest stumbling block to true independence is the assumption of capitation. PSNs need to underwrite, as a typical insurance company would, the lives of the individuals served by the health plan. How to accept risk rather than simply take discounted fee-for-service remains a formidable challenge. Other information needed to develop PSNs includes

- Models for designing the most competitive delivery system from individual organizations like Mental Health, Inc., to multiple groups blended together

- Barriers and resistances to designing or redesigning a system, including the general reluctance of most individuals to embrace change
- Legal structures for PSNs such as limited liability corporations, which allow independent organizations to act together while maintaining their independence
- Business plan design, including specific business objectives to be carried out in sequence by specific dates
- Policies, procedures, and regulatory compliance requirements for personnel management, benefits, and compensation for PSN staff
- Implementation of affiliation and cooperation agreements to link independent providers
- Marketing strategies and plans
- State and national statutes and regulations affecting behavioral and general medical health care providers
- The criteria and requirements for accreditation by national organizations

Therapists may hire specialists or administrators to assimilate and apply these ideas, but any therapists wishing to have a controlling influence on the direction of their organizations probably need to have knowledge of these and related legal-economic issues.

In April, 1996, a World Wide Web site on managed care reported data collected from 172 PSN groups from all areas of the country. Across all types of providers, PSN organizations are building management structures to compete with managed care companies.

- 85% had centralized administration
- 76% offered 24-hour service
- 38% had a computerized information system
- 53% had an outcomes measurement program

In addition, more than half the groups surveyed had formal marketing strategies, credentialing, and quality assurance programs. More than half the groups in the survey were formed in the last 5 years. Few offered a full continuum of care: Only 9% had partial hospitalization, 20% provided inpatient care, 35% had intensive outpatient services, and 14% had formal links with medical/surgical services. About half the groups did not have regular staff to handle key functions such as business administration, marketing, quality assurance, and outcome research (Group practice survey, 1996).

Despite the promise offered by PSNs to return care management to providers, many economic barriers remain to be hurdled. As long as provider groups must deal with carved out behavioral health firms, they are vulnerable to MCO decisions that reduce the percentage of payer dollars paid to the PSN, thereby giving increasing profit margins to the carved out MCO. Although its findings were not clearly substantiated, a 1996 report suggested that PSNs receive only 25-30% of the mental health dollars paid by employers to carved out MCOs ("Premiere Group Practices," 1996). Fees paid to PSNs can go lower even as PSNs perform case management, quality assurance, and utilization management internally, in this way taking over the functions of the MCO. Unfortunately, some payers, seeing the rates paid by MCOs to successful PSNs falling, may simply accelerate the price decline to save the money for themselves. Careful political and business strategies are required to maintain the viability of PSNs in these unregulated arenas.

QUESTION THE NECESSITY OF INSURANCE COMPANIES AND MANAGED CARE COMPANIES

What do these organizations actually do besides allowing money to flow through them to providers, from which they take a percentage? Insurance companies began when sailors and firemen recognized that some of them might not come back home after duty. Each member of the unit put a set amount of money into a pool, and money was paid from the pool to any widows and their children. These pools needed administrators, the administrators needed organizations, and the organizations recruited increasingly more sailors, firemen, and others to use their services. They grew to become big companies that invested the pooled money in stocks, bonds, and real estate while also making a profit on the difference between payments to policyholders and policy income.

Insurance companies are needed by health care institutions for their deep financial reserves in those rare cases of high medical cost associated with a very expensive single treatment or a run of several expensive problems. Insurance companies can also provide software, hardware, and claims processing. They are not necessary in the long run because provider groups could take over these functions. Insurance companies can help new provider groups get started by insuring them against catastrophic losses.

MCOs that are not part of an insurance company have less value to a system than those with insurance company links because most of their efforts could be taken over by efficiently run provider groups. MCOs may need higher profit margins to survive than provider groups. One estimate (N. Cummings, personal communication, May, 1996) suggested that MCOs require a 25% margin of profit, whereas provider groups could do reasonably well at 15%. For the system as a whole, then, PSNs may be most desirable.

USE PSYCHOTHERAPY CHANGE STRATEGIES TO HELP YOURSELF ADAPT TO MANAGED CARE

Psychotherapists have gathered an impressive array of concepts and techniques that are reasonably helpful, such as facing fears, controlling reinforcers, changing thoughts, separating the past from the present, taking care of boundaries, resolving conflicts, and altering interpersonal schemas. What is good for the client should also be good for the therapist. Following are various change strategies applied to psychotherapists attempting to adapt to managed care.

Define Fears and Face Them

Many therapists fear not having a high enough volume of clients to earn a decent living. Students may not have enough experience to be on provider panels and may find themselves having to change careers. These fears are very real. Some therapists will be excluded from provider panels. Consider legal action. Some therapists simply abandon their own practices to join the opposition by becoming employees of managed care companies. This temporary solution gives rise to future fears because managed care companies usually downsize to maximize profit. Face your fears. Avoidance can only make them more intimidating. Therapists can construct exaggerated fears about managed care companies. Although some MCOs are truly evil, greedy, and ignorant, mature ones work to be user-friendly. Probe the companies.

Control Reinforcers to Control Behavior

Define your reasons for being a psychotherapist. How much does money motivate? How much money is enough? How much does helping others through psychotherapy provide motivation? How valuable are other reinforcers such as interpersonal control, professional intimacy, breaks from an otherwise lonely life, and self-healing through healing others? Perhaps, as once was the case in the history of psychotherapy, the money is not so important to you.

Change Thoughts to Change Emotion and Behavior

Therapists help clients turn crisis into opportunity, stumbling blocks into stepping-stones. Managed care could be reconceptualized as positive. For those forced out of practice or denied the opportunity to practice, constructive self-talk will include statements such as "Maybe this will turn out for the best. How can I find a new focus for my efforts?" For those remaining in practice, self-talk will include statements such as "Examine my practice skills, evaluate my marketing methods and collegial networking. Find ways to become more efficient and effective."

Separate Past From Present

The attitudes and methods of the past are slipping by quickly. The past is past. The inertia of old and comforting attitudes must be overcome. There is no quiet office life anymore; there are major intrusions. The comforting solitude of private practice is giving way to required clear definition of practice.

Strengthen Weak Boundaries
and Loosen Tight Boundaries

Psychotherapy has been diffusely defined. Its parts have been incoherently arranged. Define your practice, your strengths, and your capabilities. Define yourself and your treatment methods clearly enough for the general public to understand. Look outside your practice for people with whom to affiliate. Relinquish rigid adherence to a single model or approach. Develop a disciplined flexibility. On the other hand, perhaps you have reached your limits as a practitioner. Maybe you should try another field of work.

Resolve Conflicts

No longer a time of competition, the era of managed care requires collaboration. Work with those whom you respect to develop mutually beneficial business and professional arrangements.

Alter Interpersonal Schemas to
Alter Interpersonal Functioning

Examine your schema for working with managed care companies. How angry do they make you? Examine your schema as a psychotherapist. What script do you have for your future? How is managed care interfering, or threatening that script? What must you do to maintain your dream? How much of your dream must be forsaken? Continue adapting to change by anticipating what can happen. Create your own future; don't just respond to what others do to you. Plan for your part in the evolution of managed care. Participate in decisions about carving in or carving out. Develop and become part of integrated systems.

BE FLEXIBLE, DIVERSIFY, AND
CONSIDER ALTERNATIVES

Be willing to go where clients are—schools, nursing homes, primary care offices, jails, partial hospitalization programs, rehabilitation centers— perhaps several in a single day. Reimbursement will depend on marketplace demands for early intervention to prevent long-term expenditure. Home visits will become commonplace (Fink, 1995). Be willing to work weekends and nights. Be willing to carry a beeper for your client emergencies.

Consider Rural Practices

Therapists tend to congregate in high-income urban or suburban areas. Potential work exists in the hinterlands where people are underserved. Working in a small town means living in a small town. For some, the choice may be work in rural areas or finding some other line of work.

Work With the Severely Mentally Ill

Although many psychiatric residency training programs are closely tied to facilities run by the state, psychotherapy training programs in other disciplines have spotty contacts with the severely mentally ill. In most states, psychology training programs have little awareness of the needs of the severely and persistently mentally ill, although many state programs would appreciate the opportunity to develop liaisons to fashion training experiences that make students suitable for work in the full continuum of care provided to these clients. Will there be sufficient funds from state-run programs? These state programs are being privatized to be brought under managed care schemes. Increasingly clever clinician/managers are likely to be financially and clinically successful in this arena.

Consider Forensics

For the foreseeable future, state governments will be required to fund programs for criminals with psychiatric problems. Managed care is finding a way into these efforts but will be stymied by the fact that a judge's ruling determines length of stay and the point on the continuum of care for the prisoner. MCOs therefore cannot do utilization management. They may be able to manage such clients when the judicial system has defined the terms of their imprisonment/treatment. There is more to forensics than criminals with psychiatric illnesses. States may look for ways to wrap more services into behavioral health contracts, including foster care, child welfare, and prison services. Forensic services can include court-ordered evaluations to determine competency to stand trial, treatment to restore competency, and inpatient care for clients found guilty by reason of insanity. Providers participating in such systems will need to be trained and credentialed by organizations such as The American Board of Forensic Psychology.

Investigate Telepsychotherapy

If a group of mental health professionals is in charge of a population spread over a large geographical area, then transportation time becomes an expensive variable in the delivery of services. Clients may be reluctant to travel until the problem reaches crisis proportions. Therapists may be required to spend precious time on the road. Interactive video consultations help to solve the time/distance problem. Highly successful programs have been developed in many states including Texas, Oregon, and Montana.

Certain client groups may not be evaluated effectively with interactive video. Children and the mentally retarded are perhaps better videotaped before the consultation rather than directly interviewed ("Mental Health Applications Catch On," 1994). Anorectic clients may respond to seeing themselves on the video monitors with a decreased sense of self-esteem. Schizophrenics whose delusions involve excessive influence by television may be reluctant to participate. Socially phobic clients may be terrified by the perceived necessity to perform in front of the camera. Some clients may simply marvel at themselves or the technology and find the system to be a distraction from the interview. On the other hand, the increased interpersonal distance created by the mediating electronic technology may enhance the comfort of some clients. In addition, the reduction of available nonverbal behavior may increase the ability of some interviewers to focus on more task-relevant information (McClaren, Ball, Summerfield, Watson, & Lipsedge, 1995). The psychotherapist's face should approximate real life, requiring monitors of about 27 inches ("Mental Health Applications Catch On," 1994).[1]

Learn Standard Psychopharmacology

Research evidence has strongly indicated the effectiveness of "psychotherapeutic" drugs for a variety of "psychological" problems in-

including anxiety, depression, bulimia, and alcoholism, as well as for schizophrenia and manic-depressive illness (Schatzberg & Nemeroff, 1995). The pressure of cost containment requires that psychotherapy not be offered in the absence of pharmacological alternatives. The relationship between medications and psychotherapy can be remarkably complex (e.g., Beitman, 1996), as can the relationship between pharmacotherapist, psychotherapist, and client (Woodward, Duckworth, & Gutheil, 1993).

Learn Herbal Psychopharmacology

Nonmedical psychotherapists are prohibited by law from prescribing psychopharmacological agents. Medical degrees currently are required. Anecdotally, there is evidence that many psychotherapists who are working closely with primary care physicians tell those physicians what to prescribe for their clients; however, the percentage of therapists so directly involved with prescribing has not been studied. On the other hand, an interesting variety of psychoactive herbs—herbeceuticals—is available over the counter in health stores and supermarkets. Many of these herbs seem to possess antidepressant and antianxiety properties. For example, *Hypericum perforatum* (St. John's wort) has been described as an effective antidepressant for more than 4 centuries. In 1994, German physicians prescribed almost 66 million daily doses of preparation containing hypericum. A meta-analysis of 23 randomized clinical trials including a total of 1,757 outpatient clients with mild to moderately severe depression done in Germany suggested that hypericum was more effective than placebo and compared well in efficacy to standard antidepressants (Linde et al., 1996). None of the studies lasted longer than 2 months, so longer studies are needed. In addition, several of the comparison studies used lower doses of standard antidepressant than are conventionally employed (DeSmet & Nolen, 1996); nevertheless, at doses of 300 mg of hypericin extract three times a day, it appears that clients have little chance of experiencing side effects and a reasonable chance of being helped to recover from mild to moderately severe depression. Other promising herbal agents include kava extract for anxiety, ginkgo biloba for memory problems, and various amino acids for anxiety and depression (Murray, 1996).

The legal ramifications of therapist suggestions that clients take herbal remedies are not at all clear. In this litigious society, someone could sue for anything. It appears likely, however, that sometime in the not so distant future, some herbeceuticals will be endorsed for medical practice because the U.S. Food and Drug Administration has made it clear that it wishes to support efforts to develop FDA approval for these substances (N. Israelson, former FDA lawyer, personal communication, September, 1996). A window of opportunity for therapists now exists to utilize centuries-old remedies for anxiety and depression in their practices.

Find Psychotherapy Niches

A relatively small number of experienced clinicians have developed strong reputations that generate a constant source of referrals. Most clinicians do not have this resource on which to draw.

Perhaps psychotherapists have become "addicted" to third-party reimbursement and have failed to see other opportunities. Private pay may become a strong component of psychotherapy practice if potential clients learn of its value, including privacy, choice, and control. With creative imagination, therapists may discover new unmanaged services to clients, business that can pull them away from third-party dependence and other professionals (see Ackley, 1997). Consider EAPs, work site crisis intervention contracts, mental health home care, job reentry services, and substance abuse services for Department of Transportation contracts (Hutchins, 1995b). Evaluate mediation services for couples in divorce and for families torn apart by accusations of sexual abuse (Hutchins, 1995a).

A network of Christian inpatient and outpatient facilities has extensive advertising campaigns, radio programs featuring psychiatrists and psychologists, a 1-800 number, and the support of area churches who are often willing to pay fees their parishioners cannot afford. Some of these programs have very few female therapists, but many clients request female therapists. If a woman also has a PhD, she is therefore able to more readily collect insurance payments. Therefore, a female therapist with a PhD could find a viable niche in these settings (Melanie Wilson, personal communication, December, 1995). Similarly, some churches want only a member of their faith to be seeing their congregants.

Try Primary Care Collaboration

Build on the potential "medical cost offset" of mental health treatment. Devise and test specific questions. For which clients with which problems are primary care physicians, psychiatrists, and psychotherapists more cost effective? More specifically, which type of client with what kind of problem is best treated by what kind of primary care physician, psychiatrist, or psychotherapist?

In addition, the Pew Commission recommends that all health professionals enlarge the scientific bases of their educational programs to include the psycho-social-behavioral sciences and population and health management sciences in an evidence-based approach to clinical work. A potential niche is that of medical professional education.

Participate in Employee Rights Litigation

With increasing frequency, attorneys who represent clients with employment rights disputes are utilizing the services of psychotherapists throughout the course of legal representation, particularly in preparing individuals for deposition or trial, but also in the popular alternative dispute resolution process of mediation. A psychotherapist may assist an individual in dealing with the loss of employment and the difficulties in seeking reemployment. At the other end of the spectrum, a psychotherapist may serve as an expert witness at trial, testifying, for example, to the clinical effects of discrimination at work.[2]

Consider Learning Organizational Consulting

Increasingly more training programs in business schools and other academic settings are producing consultants who view organizations as living entities struggling to maintain themselves and to grow. Many of these consultants use analogs of psychotherapeutic concepts to "put the organization on the couch" (Diamond, 1993). At the outset, the organizational consultant is an action researcher (ethnographer, participant observer, clinical researcher) who collects and analyzes data from all corners of the organization. Then, as an applied behavioral scientist, the consultant develops plans intended to resolve barriers to organizational change. Barriers and resistance to change arise from historical role conflicts, conflicting values, and underlying inaccurate assumptions of participants.

LOOK TO THE TECHNOLOGICAL FUTURE—
ELECTRONIC MANAGEMENT SYSTEMS

As radical and swift as are the changes being brought by cost containment, the changes heralded by new information technologies are even more swift. In attempting to keep steady by constant change, therapists are expanding their knowledge and use of cyberspace.

Information systems accelerate the flow of data beyond anything telephone and written records can do. Information systems can combine financial and clinical data into highly useful guidelines for practice. Earlier information systems simply tracked money flow (accounts payable, accounts receivable, payroll, billing), as well as scheduling and registration. These systems did not take into account quality of services, access (appointment wait time, percentage of covered population using service), or utilization rates (the cost per service or cost per provider). Newer management systems combine the financial and client systems with clinical management to include quality measures (outcomes and client satisfaction) and utilization measures, as well as an electronic medical record. By merging these functions into one database, managers acquire rapid and specific feedback about group and individual provider performance. For example, how does the utilization rate of lives covered by one contract compare with national norms for similar populations? Such data allow managers to use historical and comparative information to model low, medium, and high utilization scenarios for variables such as practitioner productivity, personnel costs, and overhead rates (Trabin, 1995).[3]

THE ONLY CONSTANT IS CHANGE

Therapists are confronted with a quickly changing social-political-economic environment. The pace is dizzying. Careful analysis of trends and options, without the exasperation these forces can stimulate, will increase the likelihood of successful adaptation.

NOTES

1. For interviewing purposes, telepsychotherapy requires little more than accurate sound transmission. The clearer the visual image the better, but therapists seem to depend more on auditory than on the supplementary visual information. The technology for visual and auditory transmission continues to achieve higher quality at less expense. The least expensive arrangement involves a modem, computer, and small camera mounted on the video monitor. The major problem with this arrangement is the small number of transmissible frames per second. At 25-30 frames per second, client movement appears broken; this technology therefore is inadequate for observing jerking movements of the head and neck. In addition, poor image resolution may create a distracting glare from the faces of dark-skinned clients, especially in artificial light (McClaren et al., 1995). These systems should soon be available for use by the general public to add to current auditory telephonics. Because transmission takes place over ordinary phone lines, confidentiality easily can be compromised.

The more expensive systems (costing between $30,000 and $50,000 in 1995) have larger video monitors (at least 25 inches); can create both interactive and still images; have more frames per second to prevent (not eliminate) broken movements; have two video monitors (one for local viewing to see what the distant site sees and one for the remote image); have a touch panel to control the system, including zoom and wide angle capacity; and have a digital phone line or other connection between the sites to maintain rapid transmission as well as confidentiality.

A survey of telepsychiatry in the United States (Brown, 1995), found that most psychiatric problems can be diagnosed and managed by interactive video. Exceptions include acutely suicidal clients and decompensated clients with borderline personality disorders or other highly emotionally charged clients. If interactive video is used with such clients, another mental health provider must be in the room with the client.

One of the obstacles to full-scale implementation of telepsychotherapy is the question of reimbursement. The question will likely be settled quickly through managed care pressures. Consider the fact that in some states Medicaid pays for transportation to the treatment site and that some Medicaid recipients are likely to make appointments simply to have their mileage paid for a trip to a bigger town. Telemedicine permits direct client contact without mileage costs. On another front, the state of Montana has developed a highly successful telepsychiatry system in response to its sparse population spread over a very wide area. Insurance companies, recognizing that minimum preventive care remains a good investment against hospitalization, appear to be willing to pay for the service.

Although interactive video has been shown to receive high levels of both client and therapist acceptance (McClaren et al., 1995), some clinicians express initial apprehension. Some discomfort may arise from fear of the unknown. Other users may transfer their difficulties with telephone interviewing to interactive video. Occasionally, clinicians report that they cannot address sensitive interpersonal issues as effectively, perhaps because of the interpersonal distance created by the intervening technology. Others are concerned that their clients may be irritated by this apparent barrier to more direct contact.

Interactive video does not equal face-to-face interviewing; however, it provides a remarkable facsimile. My own experience with interviewing has been quite positive, although accompanied by several instances of technical difficulties (e.g., the sound did not work for a while). At the end of one interview with an unfortunate 52-year-old woman with long-standing generalized anxiety disorder, we both felt the impulse to shake hands, which we accomplished by extending our hands toward each camera and moving them up or down. That visual gesture communicated a significant degree of mutual appreciation.

2. Tips for employee rights involvement

a. There are time limits inherent in every legal claim. If clients believe they have been treated differently from others similarly situated, advise them to seek legal help immediately. For example, under Title VII of the 1964 Civil Rights Act, which prohibits discrimination on the basis of race, color, national origin, religion, or sex, one must file an administrative charge within 300 days from the perceived unlawful employment practice.

b. Do not automatically give extensive personality tests. The results of such testing are obtainable by the employer and can be used to defend against an otherwise valid claim. Frequently, an employer will argue that some personality defect precludes the individual from getting along in the workplace.

c. Taking extensive notes as to the individual's background can also provide an employer with an escape from liability. The employer may argue that some other event in the individual's life was more traumatic and is more responsible for any harm suffered than was the unlawful employment practice.

d. Keep the individual grounded in reality. Not every legal claim results in a multimillion-dollar verdict. Not every legal claim even results in a trial; in fact, 95% of all such litigation is settled before trial. It is important to remember that there are many means of resolving a dispute.

e. The law imposes a duty to mitigate damages. Encourage the individual to seek reemployment as soon as possible.

f. At a time when therapy is most needed, many individuals with employment claims are not able to afford it. They most likely lost their insurance when they lost their jobs. If you are acting only in the capacity of a treating practitioner, not an expert, consider working on a partial or complete contingency basis, taking your fee from any settlement or verdict (from Christine Masters, Esquire, personal communication, September, 1996).

3. The ideal information systems for behavioral health care providers integrate the financial and clinical services into one format. The following components help to create an ideal system (Maloney, 1996).

a. Electronic medical records and central client registration, including tracking of all client services. These elements are necessary for efficient billing.

b. Quick on-line access to client eligibility information and treatment history by authorized personnel anywhere within the integrated system. Any client entering the system must be checked for eligibility for treatment to proceed; then treatment history and current providers can be accessed. For example, a therapist sees an adolescent boy who had been doing well in school until he entered 6th grade. His parents did not know what was happening. He had confided in his mother regularly, and now he was withdrawn. He refused to do his schoolwork, preferring to listen to the radio, play computer games, and watch TV. He did not seem to care about school, but his appetite was good and he seemed to have his usual amount of energy. He did seem more irritable than usual. They could not figure out what was wrong.

He took some computerized tests, which suggested mild depression but nothing else. The therapist linked up to the school's computer, with parental permission, to review his grades and other records. He tested well on most standardized measures each year, including this year; however, his grades had plummeted. One teacher noted that he was late to class, particularly after recess, and another noted lateness after lunch. The therapist then e-mailed the playground supervisor, who reported that several students were noted to visit a van at the edge of the playground. They suspected some drug sales.

When the therapist confronted the child with this evidence, he admitted to smoking cigarettes and trying cocaine and other drugs. He also was buying vodka from one of his new friends in the van.

c. On-line provider matching, or automated match of client with the closest appropriate provider. A possible scenario: A client calls feeling depressed. A computer, through interactive voice response technology (IVR), requests information. With this method, clients dial a central phone number, listen to questions posed by the computer, and respond by pressing buttons on a touch-tone phone. As the basic symptom list is reviewed, the computer program checks eligibility and then currency of demographic information, including home and work locations, as well as previous treatments, current medication use, primary care physician, previous mental health providers, and past history. When the closest appropriate provider is determined, the computer makes an appointment and generates an encounter form at the referred-to location, in this way relieving the client as well as the staff of making yet another call. The symptom checklist completed at the time of the initial contact can be used as a baseline for changes initiated by treatment. With the client's permission, a copy of the intake summary is sent to his primary care physician. A prior authorization form for two sessions of assessment is also sent to the provider.

In addition to symptom checklists, forward-looking psychotherapy practices may incorporate data from instruments that provide therapists with clear information about client reactance levels (Beutler, Wakefield, & Williams, 1994), as well as readiness to change (Prochaska, DiClemente, & Norcross, 1992).

We also may see a "Universal Managed Care Assessment Form" that is used across plans and easily reformats notes or dictation. Assessments and treatment plans may be first reviewed by an "Automated Case Manager" by matching ratings on symptoms, daily functioning, and interpersonal relationships to preprogrammed levels of care and treatment guideline criteria. If the case is relatively simple and fits the automated criteria, then authorization for sessions immediately follows, relieving clinicians and staff of the tedious, error-prone system of fax, telephone calls, and waiting (Trabin, 1995).

d. Centralized scheduling and client flow tracking for services provided throughout the enterprise and/or community to ensure that appropriate resources are available when needed and prevent over- or underutilization of resources. Continuous feedback loops operate to predict where excess activity is taking place and where the system is being underutilized, in ways that help continuously redesign the manner in which business is being conduced.

e. Menu-driven interfaces with voice recognition, touch screen, and point-and-click interface options to simplify data input and ensure that data (especially clinical data) are collected in a manner that aids analysis and trending. When inputting data from a client visit, the therapist can add data points, type in brief answers and new developments not covered by the programs, and be reminded of the trends of developments in the past. Symptoms of depression, for example, can be tracked individually or in a cluster, marital and work functioning can be charted, and lessening of specific psychotherapeutic problems from a standardized list of psychotherapeutic strategies can be followed (e.g., a degree of lessening of agoraphobic symptoms by facing fear).

f. On-line practice guidelines maintained and continuously updated as new practice information is obtained from prior use of the guidelines and research findings. These practice guidelines are the natural result of integrating financial risk management and clinical decision making.

g. Greatly expanded behavioral health care information, accessible to the membership electronically, without face-to-face intervention of a therapist (self-help and demand management tools). The medical informatics movement will vastly increase consumers' ability to manage their own health care. Consumer behavioral health informatics offers a psychological spreadsheet for people experiencing high-stress life events (from a company called Therapeutic Learning Systems), as well as computer-assisted psychotherapy for psychodynamic therapy (Interactive Health Systems/Gould Center) and for cognitive therapy (J. Wright, personal communication, September 12, 1997).

Mental health professionals are likely to play several different roles and will use electronic communications for various purposes. They will act as *facilitators* by providing information not only by telephone but also by e-mail rather than requiring office visits for exchange of information that can be achieved more efficiently by these other means. Clinicians could also help to generate new self-help groups to which to refer people. For serious and chronic problems, therapists can act as *partners* for clients, families, and other health professionals by incorporating electronic communications into office visits. On-line self-help groups appeal to those with chronic illnesses that prevent them from attending face-to-face meetings or have rare diseases. More rarely, therapists may act as *authorities* in those crisis situations in which the client is incapacitated. The times are shifting. At one time, people tended to ignore their own health until it failed, then counted on physicians to save them because only they understood medicine. Now, health informatics is providing individuals with tools, skills, information, and support to play the role of primary care practitioner in the emerging health care system (Ferguson, 1996).

h. Standard tools for measurement of client progress and outcomes. Data are collected at assessment, during treatment, and posttreatment, usually including self-reported symptoms, quality of life, work and social functioning, and clinician-rated severity of function. Billing also might be streamlined through universal billing forms and codes so that payments can be electronically deposited in bank accounts, within a few days of approval. If problems arise, software can identify the error, quickly report it to the provider, and have it corrected within days instead of months. To get there, managed care leaders, as well as providers, will have to agree to set and abide by specific information system standards (Trabin, 1995).

i. A provider profiling system that includes risk-adjusted utilization profiling, client satisfaction, outcome measures, and practice guidelines compliance analyses. With sufficient input and software, individual therapists can be easily profiled along these dimensions. Many clinicians are likely to balk at the use of any such systems. The acquisition of data about clinical outcomes, quality of the therapeutic relationship, and client satisfaction is likely to pose a threat to clinicians whose performance may be less than average. Outcome data truly may be a threat to their employment. The notion of data itself will be difficult for those clinicians who see psychotherapy as more an art than a science. Unfortunately, for those with this perspective, the vast majority of psychotherapists will be functioning in an environment that defines their service as a "product" composed of two features: quality of outcome and cost. Without data on quality and cost, providers have no "product" to sell (Brown & Korn-mayer, 1996).

j. Mobile computing interfaces to ensure that access to the system is available when required in the clinical process. For example, a clinician is beeped about a client in crisis. Before returning the call, the clinician uses her laptop computer modem to access up-to-date clinical data on the client, including medications and physician visits as well as data on functioning and symptoms.

k. Comprehensive contract management features to accurately track cost and utilization across many contracting options. Behavioral health financial rules across managed care companies tend to run parallel with those of general medicine/surgery, but to differ from them. Keeping track of these differences can be extremely time-intensive for billing co-ordinators. Copayments differ, and methods to request additional sessions and gatekeeper requirements need to be tracked. Behavioral health billing systems will greatly benefit from software programs handling these questions.

9

Psychotherapy in the 21st Century

C ost containment has forced therapists to reconceptualize psychotherapy practice by directing our attention toward the future of each client contact. One hundred years of emphasis on theory and process has been replaced with an insistence on outcome measurement as it relates to the intentions of health care payers. Psychotherapy has now come to be viewed as a technology designed to achieve specifiable results. These results fall into two broad categories: client improvement and cost savings.

The title of this book includes the phrase "cost containment" because here, on the cusp between the 20th and 21st centuries, payers have been emphasizing cost savings from which MCOs profit. The political pressures being exerted by providers and consumers, however, are beginning to prompt passage of laws shifting the balance toward increasing quality of care.

As a technology, psychotherapy resembles a machine on an assembly line dedicated to producing specific products. Psychotherapists seeking to win approval for their requests for more sessions from MCOs hold increasingly clearly in mind that outcomes dictate payment.

PSYCHOTHERAPY POLICY
OUTLINES OUTCOMES

The policy objectives of payers influence what they will pay psychotherapists to do. MCOs and payers devoted simply to cost savings and
profits will limit the number of sessions they will authorize as much as
they can. Payers and their MCOs who wish to help mentally ill clients
to regain normal function will rely on measures of normal and abnor-
mal functioning (Jacobson & Truax, 1991) to determine the degree of
medical necessity for treatment. They will be managing care, not just
costs. Some payers will strive to manage the health of specific populations and therefore will pay mental health professionals fees to maximize the health of their covered lives. They will take into consideration
not only the effects of therapy on the functioning of individual clients
but also effects on the workplace, the family, and health care. Psychotherapists are then also more likely to operate as agents of prevention
and early intervention as well as providers for the seriously disturbed.

OUTCOMES, OUTCOMES, OUTCOMES

Psychotherapists now sell outcomes as products. Psychotherapy is fu-
ture-oriented; its intent is to help clients do something positive for
themselves after they leave the office. The aims of most psychotherapy
relationships fall into six categories. In the list below, an example is
given for each.

1. *Crisis stabilization.* A person is distraught because his wife has
   suddenly left him for another man.
2. *Symptom reduction.* A person has been depressed for several
   months, which has limited his work and social functioning.
3. *Long-term pattern change.* A woman repeatedly develops intimate
   relationships with abusive men.
4. *Maintenance of change, stabilization, and prevention of relapse.* A
   woman with chronic medical disease, a disabled husband, and
   recurrent depressive episodes requires continuing support to
   help maintain current functioning.

Table 9.1   Sample Questions From Treatment Outcome Profile

Quality of Life
  1. I am satisfied with my life.
  5. I have supportive friends.
  9. I enjoy my leisure time.

Symptoms
11. I have feelings of hopelessness about the future.
15. My heart pounds and races.
19. I feel that I am being watched by others.

Social and Work Functioning
20. I have recently had a physical fight with someone.
24. I am able to get around in the community on my own.
27. I am functioning well at my work/school.

Treatment Satisfaction
28. I feel better after receiving treatment.
32. Treatment staff spent enough time with me.
35. My privacy was respected.

  5. *Self-exploration.* A person with reasonably good social and work functioning wants to understand himself more fully.
  6. *Development of coping strategies to handle future problems.* A person learns to handle emotions that increase the likelihood of wanting to drink alcohol excessively but wants to generalize this coping strategy to other situations.

These aims could be matched to payer policy when there are clear payer policies with which to be matched.

Outcomes require measurement. The domains of outcome measurement have become reasonably well accepted. They include symptoms, quality of life, social and work functioning, and satisfaction with the provider. The Table 9.1 contains specific questions from one such instrument, the Treatment Outcome Profile (Holcomb, Parker, & Leong, 1997), covering each of these four domains to illustrate the probes into these areas. Another example is OQ-45 (Kadera, Lambert, & Andrews, 1996).[1]

For the payer and MCO, a very simple question follows: How many sessions are necessary to obtain the desired (measurable) outcome? Currently, most therapists cannot answer this question. The use of instruments like these is preparing the possibility of such predictions.

You may fear measurement of outcomes, but keep in mind that academics and practitioners are doing the same thing—evaluating effectiveness. Academics call it research; practitioners may call it program evaluation. Most therapists can recognize when a client is improving. Outcomes measurement try to quantify these changes. There is the chance of personalized scrutiny, and there is the potential for being unjustly excluded from a panel, but for your group, the aggregate data provide trends that predict the future needs of clients and the success of the group.

PREDICTING OUTCOME

The practice of psychotherapy takes place in the real world, in the lives of clients and their social networks. Psychotherapists only help their adaptation. Several factors contribute to outcome variance.

- Client readiness to change (Prochaska, DiClemente, & Norcross, 1992)
- Severity and chronicity of problem(s)
- Strength of social network (Bankoff & Howard, 1992)
- Matching of therapist style to client reactance levels (Beutler & Consoli, 1992)
- Strength of the working alliance (Horvath & Greenberg, 1994)
- Number of sessions (Howard et al., 1986; Kadera, Lambert, & Andrews, 1996; Lambert, 1996; "Mental Health: Does Therapy Work?," 1995)

Variables like these can be accumulated into "expectancy tables" that, like the actuarial tables of insurance companies used for predicting life expectancy, could predict outcome from an accumulating database. These expectancy tables can help therapists and MCO case managers formulate the number of dditional sessions necessary to reach a desired outcome. For example, a client in crisis who is ready to change and has a supportive social network may be predicted to require 3 sessions to achieve a desired outcome, whereas a client who has been dysthymic for 4 years, currently has major depression, has no social support, and is doing poorly at work may require at least 24 sessions. In addition, data taken during the course of treatment could allow therapists and case managers to adjust the estimate up or down. For example, a strong working alliance and a rapid response to antidepressant medication are likely to reduce the predicted number of sessions for the client with double depression (both dysthymia and depression).

Establishing the database for these predictions means collecting information from thousands of clients at regular intervals in large naturalistic studies undertaken by collaborating MCOs, perhaps with the support of the National Institute of Mental Health, using agreed upon data collection instruments and protocols. In the meantime, therapists will increase their acceptance by MCOs by attempting to predict numbers of sessions based on desired outcome using crude forms of expectancy tables (Lambert, 1996).

DISMANTLING AND REASSEMBLING
THE PSYCHOTHERAPY MACHINE

Highly influential researchers (Task force on promotion and dissemination of psychological procedures, 1995) argue that the data to guide psychotherapeutic activity under managed care are already here. As described in Note 3 of Chapter 6, a great deal of effort has been expended to demonstrate that specific forms of psychotherapy that require the therapist to follow reproducible technical guidelines can be applied to the clinical setting. These Experimentally Validated Therapies (EVTs), primarily variations of cognitive and cognitive behavioral therapy, have much to recommend them. Unlike therapeutic approaches that are haphazard, undirected, and unplanned, EVTs offer clear schemes for psychotherapists to follow.

EVTs nevertheless suffer the same criticism as pharmacotherapy clinical trials in that they do not represent clinical reality (Fensterheim & Raw, 1996). Like pharmacotherapy trials, at least in the treatment of depression, the overall improvement rates are often in the 50% range (Frank et al., 1993), and this result has taken place under controlled research conditions. In the real clinical world, clients do not fit into easy diagnostic categories and do not respond as readily in the standard ways. In addition, psychotherapy process research has a long tradition of guiding practice as well and deserves a place in the dialogue about research informed clinical practice (Goldfried & Wolfe, 1996).

The psychotherapy machine needs to be taken apart and reassembled using data from research to develop the means to improve and carefully measure psychotherapy progress. This re-engineering diminishes the importance of theory and content, instead raising the importance of initial conditions such as severity of illness and readiness to change as well as short-term objectives and their relationship to outcome prediction. Short-term objectives provide the stepping-stones to positive outcomes. These intervening variables include such variables as a good working alliance (Horvath & Greenberg, 1994) and proper client-therapist matching (Beutler & Consoli, 1992). The re-engineering provides for the development of "quality indicators"—those events that increase the likelihood of a desired outcome. A quality indicator in the treatment of diabetes, for example, is an eye examination every 6 months (to look for initial changes in retinal blood vessels that could lead to blindness). Quality indicators in psychotherapy could include measurement of the strength of the working alliance and evidence that the client has been assigned homework, because some evidence suggests that clients who do homework are more likely to improve (Persons, Burns, & Perloff, 1988).

REDEFINING PSYCHOTHERAPY

Our verbal profession has created a panoply of definitions of psychotherapy, some very simple and some quite complex. The current pressures are forcing a redefinition. This new definition should answer certain expectations. It should be understandable to our constituents, which include not only MCOs but also payers as well as politicians, the media, and our clients. It should be acceptable to therapists of all persuasions. It should provide the framework for quality indicator development. The following definition fits these requirements.

Psychotherapy is an interpersonal process that moves through time. It may involve a single client, a couple, a family, or a group. Because it is a process moving through time, it can be divided into stages. During the first stage, clients and therapists establish a working alliance (the engagement stage). During the second stage, they define maladaptive psychological patterns (pattern search). During the third stage, clients move through substages of change by giving up the old pattern(s), initiating new patterns, and maintaining new patterns (the change stage). When their work appears to be completed or when a specified limit to the number of sessions is reached, they end the relationship (termination).

Many variations on this theme take place. Some clients require a supportive relationship and therefore remain primarily in the engagement stage, with brief forays into simple dysfunctional patterns and simple changes. Some are in crisis and rapidly move to change. Some take many sessions to define dysfunctional patterns.

Most psychotherapy relationships require that clients activate their innate ability to observe their own inner experiences to define patterns to change and to initiate change (see Deikman, 1983, for a discussion of the Observing Self).

Quality indicators would then include not only measures of the strength of the working alliance but also of how effectively dysfunctional patterns have been defined, how activated the observing self has become in this process, and whether new patterns are being initiated and/or being maintained.

PSYCHOTHERAPY AND PHARMACOTHERAPY: DIFFERENT MEANS TO THE SAME END?

Once we become focused on outcomes, then inevitably a payer or MCO asks whether psychotherapy is the best means to the desired outcome. Much conflict already exists between pharmacotherapy and psychotherapy as means to symptom reduction. Empirically Validated Therapies and various psychopharmacotherapies have been proven effective in a substantial number of clinical trials involving the same diagnostic categories (see Frank et al., 1993, for depression). Clients may prefer psychotherapy, and MCOs tend to choose medications, although a combination has certain additive attractions, especially when the clinician does not know which one will work best for an individual client (Beitman & Klerman, 1991).

As with many polarizing arguments, synthesis of the opposing positions often yields new paradigms (Kuhn, 1962). Increasing evidence in the treatment of schizophrenia (Hogarty et al., 1991) and recurrent unipolar depression (Frank et al., 1990) demonstrates the value of family therapy for schizophrenia and interpersonal therapy for recurrent depression in preventing relapse. Psychotherapy changes the brain if it is effective, and pharmacotherapy changes thinking and emotional patterns if it is effective (Murphy, Simons, Wetzel, & Lustman, 1984).

Pharmacotherapy can inform psychotherapy. Psychotherapists might ask their clients who have been successfully treated with antidepressants[2] a simple question: What do the pills do to your thoughts? There has been no systematic study of this question, but I have asked several hundred physicians in a variety of audiences this same question. They all report the same general observation. Their clients tell them that their worrisome, obsessive, and/or ruminative thoughts are still present, but not nearly so intense. This new state allows them to put their attention elsewhere. Psychotherapy clients also report similar results when ruminating, obsessive thoughts have come under control.

In this way, successful psychotherapy and pharmacotherapy have similar outcomes. If the pills are withdrawn, however, pharmacotherapy clients are more likely to relapse (Pato et al., 1988) than psychotherapy clients, who appear therefore to have learned something. Can therapists offer pharmacotherapy clients a means to learn how to keep their pill-induced gains without the pills? This becomes a new challenge and new area of development for psychotherapists.

TALKING WITH THE CASE MANAGER
IS NOT ENOUGH

Psychotherapists directly experience cost containment pressures in their conversations with case managers and their agonizing over treatment plan reports. Treatment plans submitted for approval of more sessions often require many details. This simple bureaucratic tool helps to reduce costs by making authorization denials easy. The therapist-author of an incomplete treatment plan may receive a checklist of potential "errors" that should be clues to the next "test" because, indeed, the treatment plan is a test of your will to complete the form, as well as your knowledge both of the client and of psychotherapy.

Details in the form spell out likelihood of authorization. Does the diagnosis fit the list in the benefit plan? Have you completed accurately each axis of the five listed for DSM-IV? If the person is high functioning on Axis 5, you may receive fewer sessions than if the person is low functioning. If the treatment plan form also includes a question about usual functioning, then a low current functioning and a high normal functioning may net you more sessions than if the normal functioning is little different from current functioning.

If you must talk directly with a case manager, you may find a full range of responsiveness. Yes, MCOs may require your office staff to answer the phone within 30 seconds, but MCOs are not so obligated until report cards on their behavior become enforceable. You may find the case manager in a meeting or, worse, be greeted by a busy signal. Once on the line, the case manager may be incompetent, uninformed, arrogant, irritable, or helpful. Some companies tape record their case-worker conversations. You may wish to report a negative interaction.

Above all, be polite. Keep in mind the intentions of MCO case managers. They are doing a job under much pressure. They are indirectly instructed to keep costs down while also attempting to help you take care of your clients. Some are polite but inexperienced as therapists and as case managers. They may not think of alternatives that you might consider. Be clever, not angry. Remember that cost savings is utmost in their minds. If, for example, you can clearly and calmly demonstrate that seeing you for psychotherapy will prevent a more costly psychiatric hospitalization, you are most likely to receive authorization.

These time-consuming, often irritating encounters will not provide you the leverage for change. You need to be part of a political movement of therapists and clients asking for redress of excesses that divert you from your helping mission. You need outcomes measures, you need quality indicators, and you need to help advertise the value of psychotherapy to numerous constituents. Psychotherapy policy needs to be articulated by us, by you and our colleagues. We cannot afford to stand by passively to let others dictate our practice. This book has outlined many of the steps to be taken.

A VERY POSITIVE FUTURE
FOR PSYCHOTHERAPY

We are immersed in a major socioeconomic shift in health care. For many, the shift has reached crisis proportions as incomes drop, and the future looms uncertain. To seek the opportunities in crisis has long been a mainstay of the psychotherapeutic helping perspective.

The world has long sanctioned interpersonal healing. Psychotherapy will survive because clients are ever in need of the supportive, empathic, unbiased perspective of society's listeners.

As new health care delivery systems, new information technologies, new medications, and new approaches to helping others develop, psychotherapists are being asked to respond, to change, and to move with these sometimes rapidly developing pressures. Awareness of these influences, as well as understanding of their motive forces and the details of their operations, can be integrated into psychotherapeutic practice. Here, then, is the profound change being wrought by managed care as we enter the 21st century: Therapists no longer can be effective without a clear awareness of the multiple forces influencing their practice. Harness these forces, and psychotherapy flourishes.

NOTES

1. For more information on the Treatment Outcome Profile, write to Psychology Consultants, 1001 Cherry Street, Suite 304, Columbia, MO 65201. For more information on OQ-45, write to Michael Lambert, PhD, Department of Psychology, Brigham Young University, Provo, UT 84601.

2. The term "antidepressant" is a misnomer these days because medications such as Prozac, Paxil, Zoloft, and some of the older group such as imipramine and Elavil (amitriptyline) are useful for a variety of problems in addition to depression, including generalized anxiety disorder, panic disorder, obsessive-compulsive disorder (which responds only to those with some serotonergic effect, such as Prozac, Paxil, Zoloft, and Anafranil), social phobia, some posttraumatic disorder, and bulimia (Delgado, 1995).

References

Ackley, D. C. (1997). *Building a managed care free practice*. New York: Guilford.

The American Almanac 1995-1996. (1996). Austin, TX: The Reference Press.

American Psychiatric Association. (1996). *Diagnostic and statistical manual of mental disorders* (4th ed.). Washington, DC: Author.

Anderson, D. F., & Berlant, J. L. (1993). Managed mental health and substance abuse services. In P. R. Kongstvedt (Ed.), *The managed health care handbook*. Gaithersburg, MD: Aspen.

Applebaum, P. S. (1993). Legal liability and managed care. *American Psychologist, 48,* 251-257.

Balas, A., & Beitman, B. D. (n.d.) *A meta-analysis of inpatient versus community psychiatric treatment*. Unpublished manuscript, University of Missouri-Columbia.

Bankoff, E. A., & Howard, K. I. (1992). The social network of the psychotherapy patient and effective psychotherapeutic process. *Journal of Psychotherapy Integration, 2,* 273-294.

Barlow, D. H. (1996). Health care policy, psychotherapy research, and the future of psychotherapy. *American Psychologist, 51,* 1050-1059.

Beitman, B. D. (1987). *The structure of individual psychotherapy*. New York: Guilford.

Beitman, B. D. (1996). Integrating pharmacotherapy and psychotherapy: Overview of an emerging field of study. *Bulletin of the Menninger Clinic, 60,* 160-173.

Beitman, B. D. (1997). A model of psychotherapy for the 21st century. *Psychiatric Times, 14,* 45-48.

Beitman, B. D., & Klerman, G. L. (Eds.). (1991). *Integrating pharmacotherapy and psychotherapy*. Washington, DC: American Psychiatric Press.

Bergin, A. E., & Garfield, S. L. (Eds.). (1994). *Handbook of psychotherapy and behavior change*. New York: Wiley.

Beutler, L. E., & Consoli, A. J. (1992). Systematic eclectic psychotherapy. In J. C. Norcross & M. J. Goldfried (Eds.), *Handbook of psychotherapy integration*. New York: Basic Books.

Beutler, L. E., Wakefield, P., & Williams, R. E. (1994). Use of psychological tests/instruments for treatment planning. In M. E. Maruish (Ed.), *The use of psychological testing for treatment planning and outcomes assessment*. Hillsdale, NJ: Lawrence Erlbaum.

Boyle, P. J., & Callahan, D. (1995). Managed care in mental health: The ethical issues. *Health Affairs, 14*(3), 22.

Breunlin, D. C., Schwartz, R. C., Krause, M. S., Kochalka, J., Puetz, R. A., & Van Dyke, J. (1989). The prediction of learning in family therapy training programs. *Journal of Marital and Family Therapy, 15*, 387-395.

Brock, D. W. (1995). Ethical responsibilities of academic health centers in the new health care market. In M. Osterweis, C. J. McLaughlin, H. R. Manasse, & C. L. Hopper (Eds.), *The U.S. health workforce: Power, politics, and policy*. Washington, DC: Association of Academic Health Centers.

Brown, F. W. (1995). A survey of telepsychiatry in the USA. *Journal of Telemedicine and Telecare, 1*, 19-21.

Brown, G. S., & Kornmayer, K. (1996). Expert systems restructure managed care practice: Implementation and ethics. *Behavioral Healthcare Tomorrow, 5*(1), 31-34.

Burner, S. T., & Waldo, D. R. (1995). DataView: National health expenditure projections, 1994-2005. *Health Care Financing Review, 16*, 221-242.

Christensen, A., & Jacobson, N. (1994). Who (or what) can do psychotherapy: The status and challenge of nonprofessional therapists. *Psychological Science, 5*, 8-14.

Clement, P. W. (1996). Evaluation in private practice. *Clinical Psychology: Science and Practice, 3*, 146-159.

Cooper, R. A., & Stoflet, S. J. (1996). Trends in the education and practice of alternative medicine clinicians. *Health Affairs, 15*, 226-238.

Crisp, A. (1992). Long-term psychotherapy and mortality in anorexia nervosa. *British Journal of Psychiatry, 161*, 104-107.

Davis, K., Rowland, D., Altman, D., Collins, K. S., & Morris, C. (1995, Summer). Health insurance: The size and shape of the problem. *Inquiry, 32*, 196-203.

Deikman, A. (1983). *The observing self*. Boston: Beacon.

Delgado, P. L. (1995). Neurological basis of depression. *Advances in Biological Psychiatry, 1*, 161-214.

DeSmet, P., & Nolen, W. A. (1996). St. John's wort as an antidepressant. *British Medical Journal, 313*, 241-242.

Diamond, M. A. (1993). *The unconscious life of organizations*. Westport, CT: Quorum.

Dorken, H., & Pallak, M. S. (1994). Using law, research, professional training and multidisciplinary collaboration to optimize managed care. *Managed Care Quarterly, 2*, 53-59.

Elkin, A. (1996, February). *Managed care.* Paper presented at the annual meeting of The American College of Psychiatrists, Tucson, AZ.

Employee Retirement Income Security Act of 1974, Public Law No. 93-406, 88 Stat. 829 (1974).

Fawzy, F., Elashoff, R., Norton, D., Cousins, N., & Fawzy, N. (1990). A structured psychiatric intervention for cancer patients II: Changes over time in immunological measures. *Archives of General Psychiatry, 47*, 720-737.

Fawzy, F., Fawzy, H., Hyun, C., Elashoff, R., Guthrie, D., Fahey, J., & Morton, D. (1993). Malignant melanoma effects of an early structured psychiatric intervention, coping and affective state on recurrence and survival six years later. *Archives of General Psychiatry, 50*, 681-689.

Fensterheim, H., & Raw, S. D. (1996). Psychotherapy research is not psychotherapy practice. *Clinical Psychology: Science and Practice, 3*, 168-171.

Ferguson, T. (1996). Consumer health informatics: Turning the treatment pyramid upside down. *Behavioral Healthcare Tomorrow, 5*(1), 34-37, 67-68.

Fink, P. J. (1995). New careers and roles envisioned for psychiatrists as economics change. *Psychiatric Times, 12*, 54-55.

Finley, J. K. (1996). Congress acts on health bills with eye to November elections. *Behavioral Healthcare Tomorrow, 5*(3), 21-23.

Fox, D. M. (1995). The political history of health workforce policy. In M. Osterweis, C. J. McLaughlin, H. R. Manasse, & C. L. Hopper (Eds.), *The U.S. health workforce: Power, politics, and policy.* Washington, DC: Association of Academic Health Centers.

Frank, E., Kupfer, D. J., Perel, J. M., Cornes, C., Jarrett, D. B., Mallinger, A. G., Thase, M. E., McEachran, A. B., & Grochocinski, V. J. (1990). Three-year outcomes for maintenance therapies in current depression. *Archives of General Psychiatry, 47*, 1093-1099.

Frank, E., Karp, J. F., & Rush, A. J. (1993). Efficacy of treatments for major depression. *Psychopharmacology Bulletin, 29*, 457-475.

Frank, R. G., McGuire, T. G., & Newhouse, J. P. (1995). Risk contracting in managed mental health. *Health Affairs, 14*, 50-64.

Freud, S. (1900). The interpretation of dreams. *Standard Edition*, Vols. 4 & 5. London: Hogarth, 1953.

Friedman, R., Sobel, D., Myers, P., Caudhill, M., & Benson, H. (1995). Behavioral medicine, clinical health psychology, and cost offset. *Health Psychology, 14*, 509-518.

Gabbard, G. O. (1997). Borderline personality disorder and rational managed care policy. In S. G. Lazar (Ed.), *Psychoanalytic inquiry* (1997 supplement). Hillsdale, NJ: The Analytic Press.

Gabbard, G. O., & Lazar, S. G. (1997, May). *Efficacy and cost effectiveness of psychotherapy.* Paper presented at the American Psychiatric Association annual meeting, San Diego, CA.

Gabbard, G. O., Lazar, S. G., Hornberger, J., & Spiegel, D. (1997). The economic impact of psychotherapy: A review. *American Journal of Psychiatry, 154*, 147-155.

Garfield, S. L. (1994). Research on client variables in psychotherapy. In A. E. Bergin and S. L. Garfield (Eds.), *Handbook of psychotherapy and behavior change*. New York: Wiley.

Gold, J. (1996, February). *The Canadian experience*. Paper presented at the annual meeting of The American College of Psychiatrists, Tucson, AZ.

Goldfried, M. R., & Wolfe, B. E. (1996). Psychotherapy practice and research: Repairing a strained alliance. *American Psychologist, 51*, 1007-1017.

Goldman, A. (1996, September). *Combined treatment vs. separate providers*. Paper presented at the American Psychiatric Association Components Meeting, Washington, DC.

Group practice survey. (1996, April). Managed care strategies. Psychotherapy Finances. http://www.psyfin.com.

Grunebaum, H. (1985). Helpful and harmful psychotherapy. *The Harvard Medical School Mental Health Newsletter, 1*, 5-6.

Guy, J. D. (1987). *The personal life of the psychotherapist*. New York: Wiley.

Health Care Financing Administration. (1996). *Health care financing review*. Baltimore, MD: U.S. Department of Health and Human Services.

Hemmersbaugh, D. (1995, December). Practice strategies for MFTs. *Family Therapy News, 26*, 15.

Hersch, R. G. (1994). Mental health's contribution to the financial performance of a utilization management program. *Managed Care Quarterly, 2*(2), 71-78.

Hirschfelder, D. L. (1995). *How to evaluate a managed care contract*. Chicago: American Medical Association.

Hogarty, G. E., Anderson, C. M., Reiss, D. J., Kornblith, S. J., Greenwald, D. P., Ulrich, R. F., & Carter, M. (1991). The Environmental-Personal Indicators in the Course of Schizophrenia (EPICS) Research Group: Family psychoeducation, social skills training, and maintenance chemotherapy in the aftercare of schizophrenia. II: Two year effects of a controlled study on relapse and adjustment. *Archives of General Psychiatry, 48*, 340-347.

Hoke, L. A. (1989). *Longitudinal patterns of behaviors in borderline personality disorder*. Unpublished manuscript, Boston University Graduate School.

Holcomb, W. R., Parker, J. C., & Leong, G. B. (1997). Outcomes of inpatients treated on a VA psychiatric unit and a substance abuse treatment unit. *Psychiatric Services, 48*, 699-704.

Hollon, S. D. (1996). The efficacy and effectiveness of psychotherapy relative to medications. *American Psychologist, 51*, 1025-1031.

Hood, R. (1996, June 2). Medicare must change soon. *Kansas City Star*, pp. K-1, K-4.

Horvath, A. O., & Greenberg, L. S. (Eds.). (1994). *The working alliance: Theory, research and practice*. New York: Wiley Interscience.

Howard, K. I., Kopta, S. M., Krause, M. S., & Orlinsky, D. E. (1986). The dose-effect relationship in psychotherapy. *American Psychologist, 41*, 159-164.

Howard, K. I., & O'Mahoney, M. T. (1996). Dose-response research provides answers. *Behavioral Healthcare Tomorrow, 5,* 44, 49-51.

Hutchins, J. (1995a, December). Barrett calls for MFT mediation for false memory families. *Family Therapy News, 26,* 21.

Hutchins, J. (1995b, December). Industry downsizing, increased provider risk, and niche marketing are trends, says expert. *Family Therapy News, 26,* 15.

Hymowitz, C. (1995, December 1). In the name of Freud, why are psychiatrists complaining so much? *Wall Street Journal,* p. 1.

Iglehart, J. K. (1996). Managed care and mental health. *New England Journal of Medicine, 334,* 131-135.

Jackins, H. (1978). *The human side of human beings: The theory of reevaluation counseling.* Seattle, WA: Rational Island Publishers.

Jacobson, N. S., & Christensen, A. (1996). Studying the effectiveness of psychotherapy: How well can clinical trials do the job? *American Psychologist, 51,* 1031-1040.

Jacobson, N. S., & Truax, P. (1991). Clinical significance: A statistical approach to defining meaningful change in psychotherapy research. *Journal of Consulting and Clinical Psychology, 59,* 12-19.

Jameson, J., Shuman, L. J., & Young, W. W. (1978). The effects of outpatient psychiatric utilization on the costs of providing third party coverage. *Med Care, 16*(5), 383-399.

Jones, K. R., & Vischi, T. R. (1979). Impact of alcohol, drug abuse and mental health treatment on medical care: A review of the research literature. *Med Care, 17*(12 Supp.), 11-25.

Kadera, S. W., Lambert, M. J., & Andrews, A. A. (1996). How much therapy is really enough? A session-by-session analysis for the psychotherapy dose-effect relationship. *Journal of Psychotherapy Practice and Research, 5,* 1-20.

Kaplan, A. (1996). Two projects study managed care's influence on psychiatry. *Psychiatric Times, 13,* 62-63.

Karel, R. (1995). Legislation on medical record access could hurt patients, says APA. *Psychiatric News, 23,* 1.

Kindig, D. A. (1995). Federal regulation and market forces in physician workforce management. In M. Osterweis, C. J. McLaughlin, H. R. Manasse, & C. L. Hopper (Eds.), *The U.S. health workforce: Power, politics, and policy.* Washington, DC: Association of Academic Health Centers.

Kluft, R. P. (1985). The natural history of multiple personality disorder. In R. P. Kluft (Ed.), *Childhood antecedents of multiple personality.* Washington, DC: American Psychiatric Press.

Kluft, R. P., & Kluft, A. (1988). The post-unification treatment of multiple personality disorder: First findings. *American Journal of Psychotherapy, 42,* 212-228.

Kuhn, T. S. (1962). *The structure of scientific revolutions.* Chicago: University of Chicago Press.

Lambert, M. J. (1996). Tracking patient progress on a session-by-session basis. *Behavioral Healthcare Tomorrow, 5,* 45, 48, 50.

Lambert, M. J., & Bergin, A. E. (1994). The effectiveness of psychotherapy. In A. E. Bergin & S. L. Garfield (Eds.), *Handbook of psychotherapy and behavior change*. New York: Wiley.

Lesser, A. (1995). Canada's fiscal woes bode ill for psychiatrists and patients. *Psychiatric News, 30*, 12.

Levit, K. R., Lazenby, H. C., & Sivarajan, L. (1996). Health care spending in 1994: Slowest in decades. *Health Affairs, 15*, 130-144.

Levitas, A. (1995, November). Managed care [Letter to the editor]. *Psychiatric News, 30*, 22.

Linde, K., Ramirez, G., Mulrow, C. D., Pauls, A., Weidenhammer, W., & Melchart, D. (1996). St. John's wort for depression—an overview and meta-analysis of randomized clinical trials. *British Medical Journal, 313*, 253-258.

Lipsey, M. W., & Wilson, D. B. (1993). The efficacy of psychological, educational, and behavioral treatment: Confirmation from a meta-analysis. *American Psychologist, 48*, 1181-1209.

Maloney, W. R. (1996). How information systems are opening the way for integrated healthcare. *Behavioral Healthcare Tomorrow, 5*, 74-76.

Mauer, B., Jarvis, D., Mockler, R., & Trabin, T. (1995). *How to respond to managed behavioral health care*. Tiburon, CA: CentraLink.

McClaren, P., Ball, C. J., Summerfield, A. B., Watson, J. P., & Lipsedge, M. (1995). An evaluation of the use of interactive television in an acute psychiatric service. *Journal of Telemedicine and Telecare, 1*, 79-85.

McIntyre, J. S., Zarin, D. A., & Pincus, H. A. (1996). The role of psychotherapy in the treatment of depression: Review of two practice guidelines. *Archives of General Psychiatry, 53*, 291-293.

MCOs report lower fees, broader services. (1996). *Practice Strategies, 2*(8), 1-3.

Mechanic, D. (1990). Treating mental illness: Generalist versus specialist. *Health Affairs, 9*, 61-75.

Mental health: Does therapy work. (November, 1995). *Consumer Reports, 60*(11), 734-739.

Mental health applications catch on quickly in telemedicine projects. (1994). *Telemedicine, 2*(7), 1, 5-8.

Meyer, R. E., & Sotsky, S. M. (1995). Managed care and the role and training of psychiatrists. *Health Affairs, 14*, 65-77.

Morgan, K. O., Morgan, S., & Quinto, N. (1996). *Health care state rankings 1996*. Lawrence, KS: Morgan Quinto.

Murphy, G. E., Simons, A. D., Wetzel, R. D., & Lustman, P. J. (1984). Cognitive therapy and pharmacotherapy. *Archives of General Psychiatry, 41*, 33-41.

Murray, M. T. (1996). *Natural alternatives to Prozac*. New York: William Morrow.

National Center for Health Statistics. (1995). *Health US, 1994*. Hyattsville, MD: U.S. Department of Health and Human Services.

Niederebe, G. (1996). Psychosocial treatment with depressed older adults. *American Journal of Geriatric Psychiatry, 4*(1), 1-13.

Norcross J. C., & Goldfried, M. R. (1992). *Handbook of psychotherapy integration*. New York: Guilford.

Osterweis, M., & McLaughlin, C. J. (1995). A framework for improving the health workforce policy process. In M. Osterweis, C. J. McLaughlin, H. R. Manasse, Jr., & C. L. Hopper (Eds.), *The U.S. health workforce: Power, politics, and policy.* Washington, DC: Association of Academic Health Centers.

Palermo, B. J. (1996, February). Capitation on trial. *California Medicine,* pp. 25-29.

Pallak, M. S., Cummings, N. A., Dorken, H., & Henke, C. J. (1994). Medical costs, Medicaid, and managed mental health treatment: The Hawaii study. *Managed Care Quarterly, 2,* 64-71.

Pato, M. T., Zohar-Kadouch, R., Zohar, J., & Murphy, D. L. (1988). Return of symptoms after discontinuation of clomipramine in patients with obsessive-compulsive disorder. *American Journal of Psychiatry, 145,* 1521-1525.

Persons, J. B., Burns, D. D., & Perloff, J. M. (1988). Predictors of dropout and outcome in cognitive therapy for depression in a private practice setting. *Cognitive Therapy and Research, 12,* 557-575.

Pew Health Professions Commission. (1995, November). *Critical challenges: Revitalizing the health professions for the 21st century.*

Physician-led MCOs acting like insurance companies. (1996, February). *Behavioral Healthcare Tomorrow, 5,* 12.

Pollack, H. (1995). The capitation contract. In G. L. Zieman (Ed.), *The complete capitation handbook.* Tiburon, CA: CentraLink.

Pope, D. (Ed.). (1997). Scientific American mysteries of the mind. *Scientific American, 7*(1), 8-110.

Premiere group practices cry foul on managed care squeeze. (1996). *Practice Strategies, 2*(9), 1, 2, 9.

Prochaska, J. O., DiClemente, C. C., & Norcross, J. C. (1992). In search of how people change. *American Psychologist, 47,* 1102-1114.

Raspberry, W. (1996, June 12). Impending health care crisis must be considered seriously. *Columbia Daily Tribune,* Columbia, MO, p. 6A.

Rush, A. J., Beck, A. T., Kovacs, M., & Hollon, S. (1977). Comparative efficacy of cognitive therapy and pharmacotherapy in the treatment of depressed outpatients. *Cognitive Therapy Research, 1,* 17-37.

Saakvitne, K. W., & Abrahamson, D. J. (1994). The impact of managed care on the therapeutic relationship. *Psychoanalysis and Psychotherapy: Journal of the Postgraduate Center for Mental Health, 11,* 181-197.

Saeman, H. (1996a, May/June). Psychologists cheer as top psychiatrist jeers managed care. *The National Psychologist,* p. 1.

Saeman, H. (1996b, January/February). Psychologists frustrated with managed care, economic issues, but plan to "hang tough," survey reveals. *The National Psychologist,* pp. 1, 9.

Sanderson, W. C., & Woody, S. (1995). Manuals for empirically validated treatments. *Clinical Psychologist, 48,* 7-11.

Schatzberg, A. F., & Nemeroff, C. B. (Eds.). (1995). *The American Psychiatric Press textbook of psychopharmacology.* Washington, DC: American Psychiatric Press.

Schlesinger, H. J., Mumford, E., & Glass, G. V. (1983). Mental health treatment and medical care utilization in a fee-for-service system: Outpatient mental health treatment following the onset of chronic disease. *American Journal of Public Health, 73,* 422-429.

Schlesinger, M. (1995). Ethical issues in policy advocacy. *Health Affairs, 14*(3), 23-29.

Schmitt, K. (1995). *An analysis of complaints filed against mental health professionals in Colorado.* Unpublished report submitted to the Sunset Committee of the Colorado State Legislature.

Schultz, T. (1995). Negotiating the contract. In G. L. Zieman (Ed.), *The complete capitation handbook.* Tiburon, CA: CentraLink.

Schwartz, J. (1996, January). *Neurology of obsessive-compulsive disorder.* Paper presented at the conference Interface Between Psychiatry and Neurology, Kansas City, MO.

Schwartz, J. M., Stoessel, P. W., Baxter, L. R., Martin, K. M., & Phelps, M. E. (1996). Systematic changes in cerebral glucose metabolic rate after successful behavior modification treatment of obsessive-compulsive disorder. *Archives of General Psychiatry, 53,* 109-113.

Seligman, M. (1995). *The optimistic child.* Boston: Houghton Mifflin.

Sharfstein, S. S. (November, 1994). Who will manage mental health care? *Psychiatric Times, 12,* 43-44.

Shortell, S. M. (1994). *The challenges of health care reform: Creating organized delivery systems.* Presentation at Integrated Service Networks Under Health Care Reform: Theory and Practice, Washington, DC.

Simon, G., Grothaus, L., Durham, M. L., VonKorff, M., & Pabiniak, C. (1996). Impact of visit co-payments on outpatient mental health utilization by members of a health maintenance organization. *American Journal of Psychiatry, 153,* 331-338.

Sloane, R. B., Cristol, A. H., Pepernik, M. C., & Whipple, K. (1975). *Psychotherapy versus behavior therapy.* Cambridge, MA: Harvard University Press.

Sobel, D. S. (1994). Mind matters, money matters: The cost effectiveness of clinical behavioral medicine. In S. J. Blumenthal, K. Mathews, & S. M. Weiss (Eds.), *New research frontiers in behavioral medicine.* Bethesda, MD: National Institutes of Health.

Spiegel, D., Bloom, J., Kraemer, H., & Gottheil, E. (1989). Effect of psychosocial treatment on survival of patients with metastatic breast cancer. *The Lancet, 8668,* 888-891.

Stearley, H. (1996, June 25). Public has lost faith in nation's medical industry. *Columbia Daily Tribune* (Columbia, MO), p. 7A.

Stearns, P. H. (1993). *The industrial revolution in world history.* Boulder, CO: Westview.

Stock, H. F. (1995). Tax equity sounds the death knell for managed care and lowers malpractice risk. *Psychiatry Times, 12*(10), 62-63.

Stone, A. A. (1995). Paradigms, pre-emptions, and stages: Understanding the transformation of American psychiatry by managed care. *International Journal of Law and Psychiatry, 18,* 353-387.

Strupp, H. H. (1997). The tripartite model and the *Consumer Reports* survey. *American Psychologist, 51,* 1017-1024.

Strupp, H. H., & Hadley, S. W. (1979). Specific versus nonspecific factors in psychotherapy: A controlled study of outcome. *Archives of General Psychiatry, 36,* 1125-1136.

Surles, R. C. (1995). Broadening the ethical analysis of managed care. *Health Affairs, 14*(3), 29-32.

Task force on promotion and dissemination of psychological procedures, division of clinical psychology, American Psychological Association. (1995). Training in and dissemination of empirically validated psychological treatments: Report and recommendations. *The Clinical Psychologist, 48,* 3-23.

Touse, J. L. (1993). Medical management and legal obligations to members. In P. R. Kongstvedt (Ed.), *The managed health care handbook.* Gaithersburg, MD: Aspen.

Trabin, T. (1995). How will computerization revolutionize managed care? *Managed Care Quarterly, 2,* 22-24.

Vibbert, S., & Youngs, M. T. (1995). *The 1996 behavioral outcomes and guidelines sourcebook.* New York: Faulkner and Gray.

Wagner, E. R. (1993). Types of managed care organizations. In P. R. Kongstvedt (Ed.), *The managed health care handbook.* Gaithersburg, MD: Aspen.

Weil, A. (1995). *Spontaneous healing.* New York: Knopf.

Wells, K. B., & Sturm, R. (1995). Care for depression in a changing environment. *Health Affairs, 14,* 78-89.

Wiener, H. M. (1994). Forecasting the effects of health care reform on U.S. physician workforce requirement. *Journal of the American Medical Association, 272,* 222-230.

Woodward, B., Duckworth, K. S., & Gutheil, T. G. (1993). The pharmacotherapist-psychotherapist collaboration. In J. M. Oldham, M. B. Riba, & A. Tasman (Eds.), *American Psychiatric Press review of psychiatry (Vol. 12).* Washington, DC: American Psychiatric Press.

Woolhandler, S., & Himmelstein, D. U. (1995). Extreme risk—the new corporate proposition for physicians. *New England Journal of Medicine, 333,* 1706-1708.

Zola, S. M. (1997). The neurobiology of recovered memory. *Journal of Neuropsychiatry and Clinical Neuroscience, 9,* 449-459.

Index